Chile's Days of Terror

Chile's Days of Terror

Eyewitness Accounts of the Military Coup

introduction by
José Yglesias

PATHFINDER PRESS, NEW YORK

Edited by Judy White

Copyright © 1974 by Judy White

Library of Congress Catalog Card Number 74-15529
ISBN 0-87348-410x (Cloth); 0-87348-411-8 (Paper)
Manufactured in the United States of America
First Edition, 1974

PATHFINDER PRESS, INC.
410 West Street
New York, N.Y. 10014

To Jurandir, Ellen, Fernando, and Dolores — who did yeoman's work in getting this book completed,

To the translators who volunteered their time and skill, and

To Comrade Tulio, born among Brazilian Communists and assassinated by the Military Junta in the revolutionary struggle of the Chilean workers.

CONTENTS

FOREWORD

Most of the testimonies in this book were given to the U. S. Committee for Justice to Latin American Political Prisoners (USLA) in Mexico City in October 1973, shortly after the first group of refugees from Chile arrived there. These Chileans, other Latin Americans, and North Americans all believe in the importance of getting the story of this coup to the people of the United States. They understand the role public opinion can play in saving their brothers and sisters who are still suffering the Military Junta's repression. But none of them could have predicted the terror and death that the first year of the military's rule would bring to the Chilean people.

A few facts and figures tell the story:

Over 350,000 workers have been fired from their jobs for political reasons, according to the former vice president of Chile's labor federation, Edgardo Rojas. Trade unions have been banned and any worker showing the least sign of dissatisfaction faces firing or arrest. Thousands of people have been driven out of Chile, forced to seek asylum or to wander from one country to another in search of a home.

The toll in human life is staggering. Church and legal sources in Chile report between 18,000 and 20,000 killed and over 65,000 jailed since the September 11 coup. Many were summarily executed. Others died from torture and maltreatment in prison. Ten to twelve thousand political prisoners still languish in Chile's jails and concentration camps.

Meanwhile, the Junta attempts to quiet international protest over these outrages by turning political prisoners over to military tribunals for judgment. The victims are being tried for the "crime" of actively supporting the legally elected Allende government prior to the coup. One New York lawyer who observed the trials put it this way: "It's really an Alice-in-Wonderland theory, and it violates every constitutional principle that anyone could possibly be familiar with."

International protest has helped secure the release of many prisoners and has stopped the torture and execution of others. As a committee that defends all Latin American political prisoners — regardless of their views — USLA tries to mobilize such support here in the United States. USLA's Chile campaign has publicized the reprisals of the Junta and the plight of its victims. It has called attention to the U.S. government's role in aiding and abetting violations of human rights in Chile. (Since the coup, Washington has provided $62 million to the Junta in direct aid and $340.3 million through international agencies in which it has a controlling interest.)

USLA has organized special action campaigns around the cases of specific victims, as well as national demonstrations to demand the release of all political prisoners and an end to U.S. aid to Chile's Junta.

Continued protest of this sort is essential to save Chilean lives. To get involved, contact USLA, 156 Fifth Avenue, Room 703, New York, N.Y. 10010.

I would like to thank the Louis M. Rabinowitz Foundation and Mrs. Dominique de Menil for their generous aid, which made it possible to prepare this manuscript.

JUDY WHITE
July 15, 1974

INTRODUCTION

At the outset let us get a couple of things straight. The Chilean militarists and their supporters convinced many who do not approve of their methods that the coup was necessary because the Allende government had brought economic chaos to the country and because it was planning to overthrow, with clandestinely amassed weapons, the democratic institutions of the country. This argument was advanced at the moment when it should have been most unpersuasive. Still, many a heist has been successfully completed by yelling, "Thief!"; and to set the record straight now seems an almost academic endeavor. What we Americans like to call the business community, and what Chileans more classically describe as the bourgeoisie, created enormous dislocations in the daily life of the country and then called on the Army to intervene for the sake of order. These dislocations were brought about by businessmen's strikes, artificial scarcities, and the creation of a black market; and when the coup came it was obvious to everyone that all arms were in the hands of the military. The lessons of the downfall of the Spanish Republic had been forgotten.

I simplify, of course, and if these abstract generalizations were all we need to know about what occurred, then any further discussion is, indeed, academic. It is better to be silent than to categorize a tragedy. Even true generalizations serve as a means of protecting ourselves from hurtful reality, and if we ask people to overcome this human instinct, then our reasons had better be compelling. I can think of no better argument for opening up the subject again than that of the people who speak to you in this book — South Americans, North Americans, and Chileans who lived through the coup. They talk about their personal histories and they speculate

about what went wrong in Chile, but in the main they tell
what they saw and what they experienced in September of
1973. "Seize the fact," said the painter Velásquez. "It is all
important." And the facts of their experiences yield much that
we need to know.

Some of the facts only emerge with full force when one knows
others that these interviewees take for granted. For example,
when they speak of the bombing of La Moneda (the presidential palace where Allende met his death) you should know
that this act is the equivalent of bombing the New York Public Library at Forty-second Street and Fifth Avenue during
the working day. When they say that under the Unidad Popular government workers and peasants were better treated than
by any other government, you should know that salary in-
creases, expanded social services, agrarian reform, and na-
tionalization of some industries were instituted under exist-
ing laws and that none of these actions were turned back by
the courts, all of whose incumbents were appointed by previous governments. The Unidad Popular brought social reforms not socialism to Chile, and the impact of these reforms
was comparable, in the American context, to that of the social measures of Franklin Roosevelt's New Deal. When anyone speaks of the economic chaos under the Allende government, you should know that for more than a year these
dislocations took place without the government's losing its
support; in fact, in the March 1973 parliamentary elections,
which the opposition expected would bring down the Unidad
Popular, the government increased its support by 8 percent.

An anxious concern for the thousands now in jail in Chile
compels the people in this book to speak urgently to us. This
strikes one immediately, and it lifts the discussion out of the
repellent morass of debate and chatter and callous reportage
into which most often journalistic reports descend. The ferocity
with which they themselves were hunted down and the brutality
with which they were treated when caught urge us to find
ways to rescue the others. It is little known that immediately
after the coup Senator Edward Kennedy introduced an amendment to the foreign aid bill then under consideration in the
Senate that recommended various actions to President Nixon
in regard to Chile. The amendment asked that the military
regime not be given any aid until it showed respect for human
rights; it urged Nixon to work through the United Nations

Refugee Commission to help political refugees in Chile; and finally, it recommended that our borders be opened to a reasonable number of refugees from Chile. The amendment was passed. Not only did the Nixon regime ignore it but it soon concluded a generous wheat deal with the militarists.

Indeed, there is need in our country to continue talking about Chile because there appear to be efforts from official quarters to have us all drop the subject. I shall cite a personal experience. A month after the coup, José García, a Puerto Rican television director working with the educational television station in New York City, asked me to appear in an hour-long program which he had obtained approval to produce. Half the program consisted of film clips edited to relate the history of the socialist movement in Chile and the events which occurred under the Unidad Popular government, which Allende headed. On the second half I introduced a taped interview with Senator Kennedy and then led a discussion about the coup with four guests. The guests invited were representatives of both the former Allende government and the militarists, Reverent William Wipfler of the National Council of Churches, and Professor James Ritter, who appears in this book. García worked around the clock each day with his small staff, and although his budget and his resources were meager, everyone felt sure that New Yorkers would at last get a good report on what occurred. If it was well received, the program might well be shown on all the network's stations.

Not the least of Garcia's problems was the close supervision he suffered from station officials. His immediate superior followed the development of the script and film in detail, and although he knew nothing about Chile or South America (while watching rushes in the editing room he asked me who Regis Debray is) he had many suggestions. "What about the women with the pots?" he frequently asked. "You have to show them." Mind you, he was a liberal, but he volunteered at every juncture the *New York Times*'s editorial viewpoint, which he by then believed to be his own, that the coup was a sad matter but Allende had brought it on himself. He also counted heavily on the appearance of a representative from the militarists to give the show balance. The militarists were smarter than he, and one half hour before we were to tape the discussion their representative's secretary called to say he could not come. Frantic appeals were made to their United Nations mission and Washington embassy, but no substitute was sent. His empty chair at the discussion spoke eloquently.

When the program was shown in New York, it received, I understand, the greatest response the station had had in a long time. The station officials were not heartened by this: they fired José García and erased — yes, erased — the tape of the show. Unlike other programs on that station it was never repeated, and colleges that called to rent the tape were refused. More important, erasing the tape ensured that it would not be shown nationally. One would think that this incident of censorship is news, but no newspaper ever reported it. *Variety,* the weekly devoted to show business, carried a big article on its front page. For them it was a show biz scandal, but it is ironical that they should have been the only publication in our country to point out that this program was the only "in-depth" report on Chile carried by television.

Perhaps the best explanation for this experience comes unwittingly from a young Brazilian revolutionary in this book. He says, "And it is important that in the U.S. there is an effective means of combatting what happened in Chile in terms of international pressure, because fascism doesn't care much about international pressure from democratic forces. In Chile there will be seen the consequences of what is happening throughout the world but very little compared to what would happen if the U.S. pressured Chile. And so I think that the workers, students, progressives, and democrats from the States have the most effective means to stop the summary executions that are going on in Chile . . . In other words, that Chile's master try to put the brakes on what's happening there. It's more than political; it's psychological. One respects the voice of one's master."

That we are not counted among the "democratic forces" is a bitter judgment for Americans to face — whether we agree with it or not — but we cannot gainsay that we are Chile's master. I do not mean to discount, as others do, the power that the South American ruling classes have on their own to obstruct or turn back social progress. Nor do I think that they need us to tell them where their real interests lie. The interview in this book that talks about the hatred those middle class women who demonstrated against the Unidad Popular showed toward the poor speaks to this point, and I have had personal experience of it in Chile myself. (At a rich home in

Santiago an urbane mine owner said to me, "We will do *any-*
thing to bring down this government!") Who is seduced and
who is the seducer is often difficult to tell. Nevertheless, what
can one answer to the question, would the militarists have
attempted their coup if they did not count on American support? Indeed, many say that they already had it during the
preparation of the coup, and the novelist Gabriel García Már-
quez has begun to document this. Certainly no one denies that
all U.S. aid to Chile was cut off the moment Allende took
office. All except military aid. This was not only continued
but increased.

This book, then, speaks to us Americans with a special
urgency. It expects no mea culpas from us, thank God, but
it asks that we look out for our fellow men. It is an account
of a tragedy— "We have lost everything we won in more than
one hundred years of struggle," says a Chilean worker— but
it does not defeat us, for the truth is always exhilarating. It
is not only Chileans who speak the truth here but also
Venezuelans, Brazilians, Argentines, and you learn in a way
no news report or history can teach you what life is like in
South America for those who want to free it from poverty and
injustice. In a manner unforeseen by the individual speakers,
these interviews provide evidence, as well, of how indomitable
people are in the face of disasters. If we listen closely, we shall
be armed for the next encounter.

JOSE YGLESIAS

CHRISTIAN

[Christian is a Chilean who was employed as an engineer at a factory in the Cordón Cerrillos section of Santiago. He was a leader of a newly formed union there.]

I will tell you what happened on September 11 [1973], the day of the coup, as I saw it. I left my house at 7:45 a.m. and met some friends on the bus who were listening to a portable radio. The announcer for the Radio Corporación was saying, "Ladies and gentlemen, at this very moment the station is being bombed. We are trying to broadcast the last words of Salvador Allende so that we can hear his impressions of the coup." We were not able to hear this because at that moment the station went dead.

When I arrived at the plant, there was intense movement among the workers, lots of running around and rumors — but nothing concrete. We decided to wait and see what would happen.

We listened all day to the broadcasts on radio and TV, but only to the stations controlled by the fascists, since the left wasn't able to get out any information — not on radio or TV, or even through newspapers. Then at about 6:00 p.m., *carabineros* [police] and air force personnel came into the factory through the back patio. We received an order for all union leaders to leave the plant. We obeyed because we did not feel that we could put up any resistance, since most of the *compañeros* [comrades] had already left the factory.

I was not a witness to the break-in, so I don't know how they proceeded, but I do know how they acted in the *población* [neighborhood] I live in, La Legua. On September 13 at 11:00 a.m., I went to see how a fellow worker and his family were doing. As I approached his home, I saw the air force break into a house opposite it. An officer went in with five or six uniformed men. After they entered I could hear the cries of the woman and her children, of the people in that house. Five minutes later the uniformed men came out, got into their cars and left. Ten minutes later they returned. This time they forced their way in with strong blows and started to shoot. Through the window I was able to see two officers shoot the owner of the house at point-blank range. They shot the woman in the leg and they struck the children. They dragged the man's body outside, put it in a truck, and set fire to the house. Five or six families were left homeless before the fire could be put out. The children— who were hurt— were left in the street; the woman was taken away in a truck; and her dead *compañero* was taken away in a smaller truck. We don't know where they were taken. A woman in the neighborhood took the children in.

La Legua was one of the hardest hit of the *poblaciones*. On September 15 in the early morning, I was told that La Legua was being bombed. Why? Because, according to the fascist Military Junta, some groups were putting up resistance. The military took this as a pretext and started a brutal repression which ended in bombing without thought for the innocent people there.

On September 17, I went to the plant to see what the real situation of my *compañeros* there was. A hundred meters or so before the plant, a friend warned me that the police were waiting to arrest the union leaders. I escaped to a nearby *población*. I went into a house with an open door and explained my situation to the woman there. She was a member of the opposition, the Christian Democrats; she had wanted the military there but was in disagreement with the way they were acting. According to her, she wanted the military to keep order but not to make blood flow. I stayed an hour and she gave me money so I could go somewhere else.

I went toward the center of Santiago not knowing what to do. I thought that if I returned to my house the military would be waiting for me there and I did not want to take the chance. So for two hours I went around in circles in the center of Santiago, trying to compose my thoughts. I was determined to request political asylum but did not know from which country — Argentina? Peru? Mexico? I decided on Mexico, remembering the traditions of that country, and it received me with open arms.

JIM RITTER

[Jim Ritter, twenty-nine, is a North American physicist trained at Princeton University and the University of London. He had gone to Chile, with his four-year-old son, upon his appointment to a professorship (funded by the Organization of American States) at the Catholic University in Santiago.]

I decided to go to Chile primarily because I was very interested in the political and social experiment that was going on there. I had just returned from England and was anxious to find out a bit about a different kind of culture.

When I arrived in February 1972, the main change in the political climate had already occurred. I was told by friends who had lived there the previous year that in 1971 there was a lot of enthusiasm for the process. Well, a lot of concrete physical changes were going on and there was almost no opposition. But when I arrived, already the rich, the right wing, had begun to reorganize itself and there was the beginning of the type of real strong polarization that became so typical of Chile during the last year. I remember the October lockout, which was an amazing type of thing to live through: to see the employers actually shutting down the factories on a mass scale, to see the doctors and the lawyers going out on strike. There was no worker who went on strike. Even those workers who were Christian Democratic Party supporters, who had voted against Allende, wanted to go to work. They saw no point in the strike. It was the rich — people who had never supported strikes in the past — who were all of a sudden demanding their right to organize — the crop owners, the bus owners — who were going on strike. And the drivers and the other people were against the strike.

At that time I also began to get more involved personally

with activities. I did volunteer work: I helped unload food—milk for children, particularly—which was not being distributed and which had to get to the children. The Allende government had introduced for the first time in Chilean history a program where every child in Chile was going to be guaranteed half a liter of milk a day. And most children, especially in the southern areas, in the rural areas, had never tasted milk in their lives since they were weaned from their mothers. And so this was, I think, very important.

I mean, you have tens of thousands of babies dying every year in Chile through diarrhea, through simple curable—easily curable for us—illnesses like that. They were still a main scourge of Chilean life in the 1970s. The absolute minimal amount of medical care that the poor people in the U.S. have always had, Chileans were beginning to get and to demand as their right as human beings during this period.

After the October strike, everyone was looking forward to the elections. The elections came, the Unidad Popular won 44 percent of the vote against all expectations. And I remember at that time the feeling was fairly optimistic. But what happened between the March elections and the June 29 attempted coup was a gradual cooling of the momentum that had been developed and the beginning of really strong demonstrations. For example, the right-wing women would come down from their houses in the Barrio Alto and would park their cars. They would come down in their Fiats and their Mercedes-Benzes and they would park them on a side street. Then they would all walk about half a block to the Plaza Italia—the main center—and then walk down the main street for two blocks with their signs, as though they had marched hungry and oppressed from the rich quarters further up in Santiago. And, you know, you have to see it, the incredible hatred of these people. I remember going out with a friend of mine who was a photographer because it was the photographer's paradise to take pictures of these people—they were more than willing to show off for the camera. These were rich, middle-class, upper-class women—the ones who have the tea parties and the garden parties. You would see their faces distorted with hatred, not so much against the actual concrete activities of the government but against the actual presumption of the poor—the idea that they could determine what was going to be done. It was a very psychological reaction. Their faces would contort with hatred and they would shout out obscenities. And that was the only thing, that was their only cry. There were no political slogans on their part. The slogans that you could hear over and over again were that Allende was a miserable homosexual and that the UP congresswomen were whores and prostitutes. That was the level at which they were operating.

Remember that in Chile during all this time there was no censorship of the press by the government. Every day I read the main right-wing quality newspaper, *Mercurio,* and I also read most of the other papers fairly frequently. I could see the change myself in the right-wing press from when I first arrived. They were in opposition to Allende but opposition on the basis that "this is a bad policy, this is economically disastrous. You have to have the people who really know how to run the country running the country. You can't have these workers coming up and deciding what to do in their own factories."

You came to the point where you had, for example, *Patria y Libertad,* the neo-fascist group's newspaper, openly calling for armed revolt by the army. They were calling for this since the paper was founded. I mean openly in their columns, saying it is time for the armed forces to make a patriotic decision and throw this Marxist government out. I've never been in a country before where papers openly published calls for sedition and for the military overthrow — by violence — of an elected government. The majority of papers and radio stations were still in the hands of the right. They had the money to buy the radio stations and the papers.

The right-wing radio stations, for example, every fifteen minutes used to say that this government had to go, something had to be done. Where were the great Chilean patriotic repositories of virtue, namely the armed forces, which in the past had always protected Chile against horrible things?

The court decisions at this time had become more and more openly class decisions in their nature. I never saw a court support a single government legal action against anybody on the right.

When the government would nominate an intervenor to come into a factory which had simply not been producing, to run the factory, inevitably, if there was a favorable local situation, the owners would go to the courts and demand that this guy be arrested. They would demand first of all that all proceeds be frozen so that the man couldn't pay the workers in the factory. You know, under this 1932 law the factory wasn't taken away from the owners. It was only being run by a government representative. So they said, "Well, yes, he can run it provided that he doesn't spend any money that belongs to the factory, or take in any money." And the judge would say, "Fine, that's right, yes." And so since one could not operate a factory without somehow selling the product, receiving the money for it, and paying the people who made it, the intervenor had to either shut down the factory and put people out of work or had to, as he was supposed to by law, maintain the functioning of the factory. So he went and sold the stuff anyway. And then, of course, the owners would go back to the judge and say that he had disobeyed a court order and should be thrown in jail. And the government would have to appoint a new intervenor and the same charade would start again.

This was used more and more as time went on. When I first arrived it was almost never done, and then all of a sudden you began reading about more and more cases of this sort. And in every case, the court would rule against the government in favor of the owners, in favor of the rich.

When the peasants owned land, the old owner would often come and hire a couple of goons. They could come in with guns and they'd try to shoot the peasants if they didn't get them to run first. The peasants would return fire. Immediately the guy would go back and the judge would then order all the peasants arrested, all of them. They'd be thrown in jail and held for six months without a trial because there was a busy court calendar. So you have all the male members of an entire village held in jail for six months, without the ability to work, without any money for their families, because the judge was a friend of the owners. They would finally be released. They would have the court case and the thing would be dismissed because there was no charge against them. But meanwhile they had been held for six months and the old owner's policy had worked out. I mean, he had managed to hit the poor and hit them hard.

And then came the unsuccessful coup of June 29, 1973. But what was interesting about that, and what perhaps hasn't been talked about too much, was what went on after the coup. Immediately after the coup was suffocated, we all went down to celebrate the defeat. There was a big mob of the workers and students and myself down in the center of town to cheer the government and just be happy that the thing had been crushed. There was a big cry around "Close the Congress" because the Congress, which was controlled by the right, had stopped every single bill the government tried to put through to change, social conditions and, in fact, it had been one of the prime instigators of support for the courts when they attacked the poor and so forth. There was a feeling of real militancy, you know, a feeling of "Look, they tried to kill us today. Let's stop messing around. We don't have to play by their rules because they've already broken them. They sent out the tanks to attack La Moneda, the Presidential Palace. They've killed twenty-two of us in the streets today." There was this feeling of anger, real anger, that not only had these people been trampled on all their lives but that now, when they finally were doing something, the right — the great guardians of law and order — were the ones who were violating their own laws and killing people.

Allende said, "I'm going to be unpopular when I say this, but I can't close the National Congress. I haven't got the power. But we can work hard to try to make changes."

So we went home and the government declared a state of emergency and instituted censorship of the press. I had a friend who worked on the Socialist Party newspaper *Ultima Hora,* and I remember her telling us what problems they had. The first day all the papers had paragraphs censored, just left blank, by the military censors. You could not refer to the attempted coup. You had to say "the events," "the recent events," "because of well-known reasons," — something like that. But then as the days went by, you noticed something very interesting, namely, that all the right-wing newspapers were no longer censored because they didn't have to be. They weren't making any derogatory comments about the army. Obviously they didn't because they were in favor of what one part of the army had tried to do. They were perfectly happy to forget about the unsuccessful coup. But the left-wing papers that tried to talk about what was going on were being censored much more. I remember that the Communist Party newspaper, *El Siglo,* had a series of cartoons. One very popular comic strip featured a little cat who commented on life and political scenes. This little cat-strip was run a few days after the coup. The first day after the coup you saw the cat looking out a window and talking, with a large, completely blank speech balloon above his head and four large blank thought balloons. Then there was the political cartoon they had every day, as all papers did, and it was completely blank.

You could attack Allende, you could attack the government. But the articles from the left press that wanted to defend the government, and say that the people who were responsible for this in the armed forces should be punished — that you couldn't say! It got to the point where *Ultima Hora* was being censored more and more: until its entire centerfold, the interior pages, was just completely blank. Finally they were just so censored that one day they announced that they stopped publishing.

You could tell the political distinctions that were being made. One paper, *La Tercera,* prided itself on carrying both left- and right-wing articles, although the left-wing articles were limited to one column per day on the third page. I remember buying *La Tercera* a couple of days after the coup and looking through it to see what was censored. I noticed that there was no censorship whatsoever in any part of the paper except for the one pro-Allende column which was completely censored.

The UP government realized the ridiculousness of the situation at this point: it had imposed censorship supposedly on behalf of the armed forces, supposedly to defend the constitutional government, and it was being used against those who were defending the constitutional government and not against the opponents. So Allende ended the state of emergency, which automatically meant the end of censorship.

In the two and a half months between that attempted coup and the coup of September 11 everyone knew the stiuation had reached the breaking point. I remember going on the September 4 march, celebrating the third anniversary of Allende's election. There were more than one million people in the streets of Santiago. A very moving sight. I brought my little son with me because I knew in a sense it was going to be the last march, that something was soon going to happen. There would be a coup; it might be defeated or it might not; and either way, things would never be the same again. So I took my little boy and marched out. He carried a little sign that said, "Chile says no to civil war." We were marching down the street, talking to the people on the march — the workers, and so on. I realized that they *also* felt the way I did. They also knew this was one of the last times that they would be allowed to go on the street. They were conscious of what was coming and they were prepared to defend the government. There was no mincing words; they were expecting a fascist-type situation to develop and they were going to fight against it. And that was that.

Then, exactly one week later, it came. You could see the activity. I remember contrasting it to the June 29 coup. It was like the June 29 attempt had been a little joke. Here was the real thing. You saw the Hawker-Hunter jets circling and bombing the presidential palace. You saw them streaking out to the working class areas to bomb factories and working class neighborhoods. And you heard heavy artillery fire back and forth across the Mapocho River a couple of blocks away. From my window, for example, I could watch an attack on a building that belonged to the University of Chile — the Pharmaceutical Faculty Building. I watched the army deploying itself in total military fashion, and then a curtain of machine gun fire opened up — for about ten minutes, a sheer curtain of sound and smoke arising from this intense fire into this one building. It finally ended by someone throwing a grenade in. There was a huge explosion and then silence. This was happening building by building all over the city.

My own building was hit by machine gun fire. I was out with my little son on the balcony and heard the crack of rifle shots, which was quite common around my area. Just then a machine gun opens up from below, hitting my building maybe one story or so above my head. That's when it comes home. You get down on the floor. You try to protect your son. You worry, "Will they kill us or not?" And with that the whole thing became very real to me.

I had wanted to stay in Chile. By then I had already stayed half a year beyond my original time and I wanted to stay another year. And I had negotiated a new contract with no problem, and even after the coup I remember feeling that I would have a chance to stay. I had not been heavily involved in politics. My sympathies were known but they were shared by the majority of Chileans. I didn't think there could be that much repression. After all, I was a professional man, a visiting North American. If anybody would be safe in the new Chile, it would be me. So I made plans to stay and to see what life would be like under fascism. But that was not all. I genuinely liked Chile and didn't want to leave. I felt that somehow it would be wrong of me to leave the Chilean friends who couldn't get out. I'd see if I could help them. So, for about a week I got rid of all my left-wing literature, all my government publications, which were suddenly subversive material, as though they were smuggled in from across the border. I got rid of my records because they had horrible things about the poor people deciding their own lives. And I really thought I was safe.

About a week and a half later — on September 23 — I was awakened at six in the morning by an announcement that the military was sealing off the entire San Borja Housing Project where I lived. We were told not to leave our apartments, not to go near the window, that they were going to do an apartment-by-apartment, house-by-house search of that area.

About 10:00 a.m. they got to my apartment. They knocked on the door. I opened it, rapidly. And ten soldiers came in with their submachine guns and they started searching. They searched all my records, all my private correspondence, all my books, my clothes. They went to every room and they asked to see my documents. I had a visa that had been expired for some time. I was trying to get it renewed. In good times it would take five or six months to get a visa renewed. No one ever asked you for a visa under Allende so you never thought about it much, but you knew it was a law. I couldn't renew my visa until I could prove that I was working, until my new contract came down. I was waiting for my new contract to come through so I could present it together with my affadavit to get a new visa. I had even spoken to the head of the observatory where I was going to work. I told him my problem. He said not to worry, just give the police — or anybody who asked — his name. They could contact him and he would say, "Yes, his contract is coming through." Everything would be taken care of. It was just an administrative problem. I was a bit nervous about being caught like that. People have been taken away in the streets for having an expired visa, but you still don't think it's going to happen to you. The soldiers saw it was expired, and I remember the officer in charge of the group saying, "Well, I'll have to take you prisoner." He wrote a number on my forearm in the style done to the Jews in Nazi Germany and wrote a number on the back of my jacket. I was given two minutes to say good-bye to my son, who I had to leave with the housekeeper, and I was marched out and held at gunpoint on the ground floor of the building until they had finished searching all the apartments.

Just about 100 yards away from where I was standing they were burning books from that area. You would see them throwing the books and the papers out the windows, and bringing them down by the elevator-load from the building I was in. Just shoveling them out, shoveling them onto a fire. I remember they invited the foreign newsmen down there. The officers and men were proudly standing around the fire while they kept shoveling more books on, watching it burn with big smiles on their faces. . . .

The soldiers—not the officers but the young soldiers—the eighteen-year-old kids from poor families who were drafted and who, of course, were the bulk of the army, would sit and read political pamphlets that were being thrown down from somebody's house. It was the first time they had ever been allowed to read them, because privates in Chile are not allowed to vote and not allowed to read political literature when they're in the army. The officers can vote and read and talk. But this was the first time many of these soldiers had ever seen a pro-government publication. What the army published and what the army officers told them in the political meetings they were forced to attend was, of course, that the Allende government was horrible, that it was a communist government. As I learned later from one private soldier, they were told that the Allende government had plans to kill *all* the soldiers. It was part of this great plot to wipe out the entire armed forces—100,000 people. The only reason General Pinochet was moving against the government was to prevent this plan being put into effect. And they believed it. They had no other material to go by.

Finally I was marched out. I began talking to some of the young soldiers who were there with me. I was just talking about who I was, what I was doing, and I got very friendly with them. They kept saying, "Well, you aren't really in for anything serious. Nothing will happen to you." And I felt very relieved, that they would know, that it was just a question of getting my new visa and everything would be fine. They talked about their own lives, what they wanted and what they thought about things. Their naivete was incredible. Most of them had come from the South, from poor, small farming families, had very little contact with political events, and were not particularly interested in politics, aside from what they had been told. They were much more interested in very basic types of things: I was from a different country, what was it like? I was working in the university, what was that like? Because they would never have hopes of going to the university.

One soldier took me back to find his superior to see if I could be released. This was on his own, simply because I hadn't really done anything. And the officer said, no, that I had to be processed through. Another one took me back to my apartment so I could give some instructions to my housekeeper, because my little son was still there. They had discussed among themselves whether he should be brought along. One said, "Should we take the kid?" And the other guy said, "Oh no, no, no, let's leave him here." And I went back again and was finally taken to the Tacna Regiment Headquarters, a regiment based in Santiago.

I remember that at this time it still didn't seem real. I hadn't been mistreated in any way. I had an interesting conversation with the soldiers. And I remember saying to myself, "I've got to remember exactly what happens to me because it really is a fantastic story to tell my friends tomorrow after I get out." That was still my attitude toward it.

We were driven off in an army truck. They loaded me in with another prisoner they had taken from the same group of buildings and drove through the streets of Santiago after curfew. That was a very interesting sight— completely dead. No people whatsoever around because you were shot for going out after curfew. Every night you heard shots ring out all the time. They were getting people who were out in the streets.

Finally we arrived at the Tacna Regiment and we were brought to a sort of waiting room where we were guarded by two soldiers, just like something out of the movies. Then we were told we were going to be interrogated. I turned over my passport to the officer in charge. My name was printed in a ledger and I was told to wait. We waited a few hours; it was not yet 8:30 at night. Finally a little officer came into the room. There were now three of us prisoners. There was an Argentine leather worker who had been living with his Chilean girl friend in the housing project and had had the misfortune of not having destroyed some Russian literature in translation. You know, novels. He was taken for that. There was a Chilean with us who was the administrator of one of the buildings. He had been taken because they had found a lot of Marxist literature in one of the eighty apartments in the building. So they took him prisoner, because he was the superintendent of the building — he swept the floor.

Then this little officer in paratroop outfit — with a black beret on his head — came in. He came over to each of us in turn. And now the whole atmosphere began to change. Up to now I had been treated either with friendliness by the private soldiers or at least with some sort of official abruptness — but nothing worse — by the officers. This guy came up screaming at us, "Get up. What's your name? What are you doing here?" And finally, when you explained for the 105th time that you were a professor, and so on and so forth, he said, "What do you know about the plot to assassinate major Chilean military leaders?" I said, "What???" He said to me, "All right, I'm going away now. I'll be back in a few minutes. I'll give you some time to refresh your memory. You had better commend your soul to God if there is a God for you." And he stomped over to the next one, where he repeated the same act. It was sort of funny. I almost laughed. Luckily I cancelled that. Finally he went out and slammed the lights off like something from a bad film, and so you waited for him to come back. I was thinking, "Gee, I wonder what he's going to do next? How's this going to come out?"

And then another officer comes in. This was the hard-soft routine that I remembered seeing so often on television. He comes up to ask us the same questions as the other guy, but he asks in a soft voice. We don't have to get up: "No, no, keep on sitting." And at the end of every answer we gave, he'd say, "Perfect, great, great," as though it were just a stupid little administrative mix-up and we'd be out of there in no time. That sort of approach. He left the lights on for us so we could read, and then half an hour after he left, the little guy comes in again. This time he doesn't say a word. He just goes over to each of us in reverse order, and while we're sitting there, he brings his hand up with an open palm and slaps us about four or five times across the face and then kicks us — still without saying a word. And then passes on to the next one and does precisely the same routine. Well, this was a bit frightening for me but it still was somehow unreal. I mean, it didn't really hurt all that much, and it was all part of the same "hard guy-soft guy" routine and you felt that nothing more was going to happen. They're not going to shoot me, certainly. I mean, they would never shoot an American. This was before I knew about Frank Teruggi and Charley Horman, two Americans who were shot. I still felt absolutely safe. They could do that amount of nastiness to me but no more, and it still would make an interesting story for later.

We waited another half hour and finally were taken out and loaded onto the trucks. I assumed we were going to the National Stadium. And I still felt, well, you got through that stage. Pretty soon you're going to get out.

And then things really started changing. We got up on the truck. And we were told to lie down on our stomachs, hands clasped behind our necks, and to spread our legs. I assumed this was to prevent escape or something. About ten soldiers got on the truck after us. And the truck still didn't start. It just stayed there. And then they started beating us. Now it was for real. The whole comic opera aspect of it was gone. I remember they would do each of us in turn. First they would kick the Chilean on my left. They'd kick him in the stomach five or six times. His whole body would sort of jump in the air with each kick. And then you knew it was going to be your turn. They were going to kick you in the stomach. There was nothing you could do. Then they'd pass on to the guy behind you, the next guy in the row. Then they would take the butts of the submachine guns and start hitting you on the back of the head and on the kidneys. They'd do this to each of us in turn. I remember my legs weren't spread wide enough for them so they kicked them more and more apart. When I finally had them all the way out, one guy stomped very hard on my ankles, about ten times total on each ankle, which really hurt. Then he kicked me in the crotch. Now I began to get scared. I still didn't think they were going to kill me, but I did think they might really damage me. I really was afraid of being maimed. That they might do. And with that, the whole thing became very real. The pain didn't allow you to play the kind of safe game I'd been playing up to then — just being an observer, a cooly detached observer, of my own plight. I began to realize that this was for real and that I was not quite as immune as I thought I would be.

Finally they started the truck and they drove very slowly to the National Stadium — about a twenty-minute ride. And the entire time they kept working us over. I remember they kept yelling at us: "Goddamn foreigners. Came down here to kill Chileans. Well, we're going to kill you. You'll see."

We got to our destination and they said, "All right, you bastards. Here we are at the stadium. This is Wonderland. Now, you're really going to see something." And they prodded us into the stadium with their machine guns, the muzzle-end this time, and stood us up against the wall. Having been beaten for the first time in my life, I now realized that it hurts for the moment and then the hurt seems to go away. You think it isn't so bad after all, but when you try to do something physically, you realize just how badly you've been hurt. We had to stand up and lean against the wall. They started kicking our feet further and further apart, all the time with the muzzles of their submachine guns at our backs. And you felt that they weren't going to shoot Americans on purpose, but maybe, just maybe, if you did something they might misinterpret, they might shoot you, you know, on the spur of the moment and worry about figuring it out later. I also realized that I couldn't stand up as well as I thought I could. I was really worried that if I slipped they might kill me.

This is a period where it's hard for me to reconstruct my own feelings because I'm removed. I'm safe. I'm out of Chile. I'm unhurt. But it had a sort of psychological effect that was perhaps the real point of it. What this maltreatment did to you before you got there was to strip away your dignity as an individual. This really did work. I felt completely powerless, completely and utterly powerless. They could do anything they wanted to you. No one would come. No big hero was going to save you. The American cowboy was not going to come over the hill. You were in there and they could do whatever they wanted to you. That might include maiming you, it might include killing you, it might include torturing you. There was nobody who was going to make it all better and fix it up. You could not even take refuge in yelling back at them, making a wisecrack, because as I found out later from people who had seen this happen, one guy who sort of broke finally was just shot dead where he was. You sort of felt this was a real possibility even before you knew about it concretely. You just accepted whatever they did to you, and it was this acceptance even more than the physical pain that really broke you down as an individual. You had to accept everything.

Finally I was taken over to another part of the stadium—
inside the stadium, not where the bleachers are, but underneath
the bleachers where the locker rooms are. We were put against
the wall again but this time we were searched. I had not even
been searched before. This "up against the wall" was simply
another minor physical maltreatment. But now the guy took
all my stuff: ripped my wallet open to see what I was holding,
checked inside of my boots to see if I had anything incriminating on me. I had gotten rid of my money when I went back
to my apartment so they didn't get to keep that as they did
with other people. My name was again entered in a ledger,
again I had to go through the same rigamarole about what
I was doing and so on and so forth. They gave me back my
passport and I was taken to the prison section.

Now in the section I was in, they were using locker rooms.
There were six in my section, each large enough to hold perhaps eleven men comfortably, and these were filled with about
180 people. You could count them when the people came out.
In fact when I arrived they couldn't even physically fit any
more people in the locker room. You looked inside and it was
packed, a sea of people, mostly just standing or sitting very
hunched up. There was simply no more room physically to
put us in, so they put us in a new section they were starting,
which was where the bleachers met the wall. Each of us was
given one blanket and told to go there. I arrived very late—
12:30 or 1:00 in the morning—so I just went to sleep. The
lights were always on. There were armed guards with cocked
submachine guns all the time, mainly pointing at you or
around you. This was the type of existence you simply had
to learn to live with. At this point I realized that this was not
going to be a one-day little piece of administrative nonsense
I'd have to go through. This was a bit more serious.

Prison routine is hard to talk about because it is the most
incredibly boring thing in the world. There is absolutely nothing to do. You get up in the morning and it's cold. It was
a very cold spring in Chile this year. And you sit huddled in
your blanket and you wait, just wait. The lights are on all
the time; the guards are there. They move around a bit but
they don't actually do much. They talk together quietly. You
can talk to other prisoners and, of course, you want to. You
want to feel somehow identified with other people. You want
to have some feeling of support. The big event is breakfast,
because it's something that happens. You're taken out. For

breakfast we were given a cup of coffee with milk and sugar and a little piece of dry bread. It was nice because you got in line. You picked up your piece of bread and you got your coffee. You sat and drank and ate — or you stood up and drank and ate — and you began to talk again. And then breakfast was over. You rinsed out your little plastic dish and gave it back and left the cup. And then you just sat there again. Then at about five or six in the afternoon we were given a little bowl of beans — hard lima beans — and noodles and another piece of bread. That was the diet you were on. It very quickly began to take its effect and make you weak. It was enough to keep you alive and to keep real intense hunger pains off, but you were always hungry, silently hungry. And you were debilitated so that you sat and couldn't even talk after a while. It was too much effort. If somebody new came in, you'd ask how he was, what happened to him, how was he tortured, and so forth. Then you just sat there.

I was personally lucky because I was taken late. I was taken on September 23. And the following day I was called out to be interrogated. But there were people who had been in my section of the stadium since September 11, primarily students from Technical University. This university had been bombed and attacked by land. A lot of people had been killed, a lot arrested and taken away. Some workers from various factories who had been taken the first day were also there. They had had *no* interrogation, not even their first interrogation. They'd already had a week and a half of enforced inactivity and prison life, as well as whatever beatings they had had before they had gotten there, and some of them had been pretty violent. I was taken out because I was an American and given my first interrogation. The man who was interrogating me was a Chilean detective from the Investigations Division. He was very proud of the fact that he had graduated from the International Police Academy in Washington in 1965. He had learned a trade. He wanted to show off his English a bit while he was interrogating me. Once in a while he would ask me something in rather bad, broken English. I was really desperate because I had talked to some people in my cell who had told me that while they had been interrogated, there were some foreigners present. There were about eight people being interrogated at a time. And beatings were administered to Bolivians and Brazilians as a matter of course. *That* was their interrogation. They weren't even asked anything; they were just beaten.

This guy just in front of me was being interrogated, and the guy just behind me was just being beaten, completely beaten by a couple of guards and by the detective. Meanwhile they continued to ask him questions about his political activity. So when I got in I was really nervous. I had no idea what this man would do. He might take a shot at me or anything. So I really tried to play a role — apolitical physics professor who came to Chile, had no political opinions, and was caught up in an administrative error. Both of which were true — not the apolitical, but the professor and the administrative error part. He seemed to believe me and he read me back a summary of what I had said, which seemed to be fair enough. I signed it and he said, "You're free." He said, "It's probably too late now to make your curfew, but you'll be out tomorrow." So my paper was taken out by another detective and turned over to the army again. I was told to wait in this line. There were two other Americans who were interrogated at the same time I was — David Hathaway and Juan Donoso — but they had not passed the first interrogation and were being held for the second interrogation. But I had been, I thought, freed, and I went out to another section where we were with the other people who had been freed during their interrogation. We were marched off to the upper concourse of the stadium, the open area where they sell soft drinks during the games, and we saw a lot of people there. We thought, "Oh, boy. All these people have been freed today and are just waiting here overnight for the curfew to be lifted again so they can leave tomorrow."

But then they started talking to you and you realized that a lot of people had been here since the first day. They also had been told they were freed, been sent to this section and just stuck there. The advantage of this section was that your interrogation had been passed. Therefore you had a bit more freedom to move around and walk and talk. The disadvantage of it was that it was freezing cold. All the windows on the front wall had been shot out by machine-gun fire so that the wind came whistling right through. We sort of shared blankets and huddled next to each other for warmth and, even so, you had to get up every couple of hours to walk around and restore some circulation and try to go back to sleep again. Here again, one noticed the same type of listlessness, tiredness. The only topics of conversation that I remember were what happened to you and what we're going to eat when we get out.

You're allowed to sit outside during the daytime in the stands and every day a list is read off in your section of those who are to be allowed to go free — really free, or so we thought. Chances were 100 to 1 of your ever being mentioned on it because they released about 100 people and 200 people came in every day. So there was a constantly increasing number of people being held in this section.

I had a chance to talk to a lot of people in this section who'd been in since the day of the coup. I remember talking to some Chilean students from the Technical University who had been taken to the Chile Stadium. That's another stadium that had been used the first week for political prisoners. And the stories they had to tell were incredible. During the first days the conditions were really subhuman. There were no blankets. And there was murder. It was done deliberately in front of you. A number of people told me that in their section the officers gave orders for the men to fire point blank and at random into the crowd of prisoners. This was when they first arrived. And this guy saw about four people drop within three feet of him. One group of army people took eight prisoners and lined them up against the wall. They hit them with rifle butts in the back of their heads, then shot them in the back. Another group of prisoners was taken out by the *carabineros*, the uniformed police, to a courtyard, but still in full view of the prisoners, and forced to run around and then they would just shoot at them. One guy fell down. He couldn't take anymore and they started beating him with their rifles until he got up and ran. Then they just shot him.

I saw the results of interrogations. I remember a Chilean worker being brought up to our section — conditional liberty it was called. He had been interrogated. The interrogation consisted of his being beaten with a rubber hose filled with cement until his back was completely black. He couldn't move. We got a mattress for him. We had only a few mattresses. We were using them for the sick and the wounded. We had to turn him over every couple of hours to prevent him from getting bedsores. We had to sit him up and feed him. The military would not take him to the hospital because there was no medical care for prisoners. Only for the soldiers. And he had been beaten, he told us, because when he was brought in for interrogation they said, "We want you to sign a confession that you were in charge of the arms in your factory, that you know where they are and that you want to tell us." There were no arms in this man's factory. He had nothing to tell them. They just beat him. This man was with us for about a day and a half and it was only later that we could get him to talk about it. Then he was taken down because, luckily, the International Red Cross came by that day. The guy from Geneva who saw him took one look at him and made them take him down to the hospital.

I remember seeing a Belgian guy being carried out after interrogation. I found out his story later from a friend who'd been in the same cell. He had come down in the days of Frei, the previous Christian Democratic president, to work and had liked Chile very much and decided to stay. He was working for CORFO, a big economic agency which had been set up thirty years ago. It is in charge of running state factories, giving technical aid, and so forth. He was a sort of middle-rank functionary. When he was arrested, it was because he was foreign and because he was a government employee. They had decided that he was responsible for the distribution of arms in Chile to the workers, which was, of course, just complete fabrication on their part.

He was taken for interrogation and he was beaten so badly that I saw him being carried out by four people. He was completely unconscious and bloody. And his two aides were being carried out after him equally unconscious, carried down to the little makeshift infirmary which did not do anything more than give you some aspirin and bandages and then send you back to the cell.

I was finally released on Wednesday, September 26, because of pressure from the U.S. A deal had been made, as I found out later. But all I know is that all Americans were taken to a section and they had a list, including three names who were not there— Frank Teruggi, Charley Horman, and a woman named Rodríguez. These were the names the American Embassy had of those Americans who had been arrested and sent to the stadium. They said Frank Teruggi had been released the previous Friday and that Charley Horman never came to the stadium. Both these men I found out later had been shot. Rodríguez, they said, was being held in the South, which I later found out was true.

We were taken in one by one for a final processing. It was obvious that we were going to be released. There was a guy

from *Investigaciones,* sort of the Chilean FBI, sitting there
and filling out forms. Now, we had to sign two forms to be
released: one was a little form saying that we had not been mistreated in any way. So I signed it. I was not going to make a
civil libertarian issue. I just wanted to be released. I was getting out with my life and so I signed. Then the other form
was even more interesting: they ask my name, where I came
from. I say the San Borja Housing Project. One of the agents
says, "You know, it really would have been a lot easier if
you had just taken these people out and shot them instead
of bringing them here. Oh well. . . ." And then he turns back
and asks me what I did. This was standard. You were always
meeting up with this type of— I don't know if it was gallows
humor. I never knew how to take it. You knew that it was
a real possibility. Well, it was a large piece of paper and it
had a large major section which said, "Statement, Confession
Excerpts" and that was left blank. And I was told to print and
sign my name at the bottom of this blank space. Again I wasn't
going to object. So they now have a blank confession signed
by me and signed by all people who have been released. At
any time they can fill in that we were down here and we killed
five hundred soldiers. With those two papers out of the way,
I was taken out, fingerprinted, photographed, taken out by an
air force major who sort of sneered at us and said, "Who
are you, the good guys or the bad guys?" We'd all been released with the proviso that we all be deported within seven-
ty-two hours from Chile.

Well, this settled the problem of whether I would stay or not.
Even in prison I had considered staying, though I think now
that was really a romantic idea, considering what happened.
We were driven out of the grounds in an official embassy car
with the air force major sitting in the front seat.

I went back to my home, back to my son who had been
fine, taken care of by my friends in a lovely way, to prepare
what I could for leaving.

OSNI GERALDO GOMES

[Osni Geraldo Gomes, twenty-three, is a Brazillian art photographer. In the two and a half years he resided in Chile he had never involved himself in that country's politics. He happened to be on the street near the Presidential Palace when the coup began. To escape the gunfire Gomes took refuge in the apartment of Bolivian friends who lived nearby. Following his arrest he spent forty-five days in the National Stadium.]

From the apartment of a friend we saw the bombing of La Moneda, but it was impossible to identify the type of planes. Helicopters flying at low height aimed at the buildings where snipers were shooting back. Those, whenever caught in the streets, were shot down on the spot. Many people were being taken prisoner and all the while military bulletins read on the radio placed all the blame for the resistance on foreigners. Through these bulletins the army urged all those who had no political involvement to present themselves at police stations. We had our passports and everything in order, but could we risk going out on the streets when they were shooting right and left?

On the third day after the coup there was no food left in the house and we learned from the radio that people would be allowed to go out for two hours in order to buy their basic supplies. Workers who had stayed in their factories were urged to return home. I had just finished taking a bath and was getting dressed when five or six *carabineros* broke into the apartment. Others had placed themselves on the stairway and the whole building had been surrounded although nothing

had happened there to justify such a measure. There had been
no resistance or shooting from any of the windows. Forced
down by beatings and with guns pointed at us, we were made
to lie on the floor face down with hands clasped behind the
neck. They searched all over the place for documents and
guns — throwing books and clothes on the floor and tearing
up mattresses or whatever they could lay their hands on, but
they were unable to find anything incriminating. While all
this was taking place they kept yelling all sorts of insults and
asking why we had come to their country to kill good Chileans
and eat their food. We did our best to explain that our documents were in order and that we were just working people.
They wouldn't even look at our passports. We were made to
get up and they started kicking us out of the place. I asked
permission to put on my shoes and shirt (since I was still
naked from the waist up), but they said that we were at war
and that there could be none of that stuff. We were taken to
a truck with other prisoners who had been gathered from other
buildings. Some of them, as we were told later, had been denounced by neighbors as having voted for the Unidad Popular. We were thrown on top of each other like animals — men
and women alike. All this, of course, during constant beatings
and cursing. We were taken to the Second Police Station and
our names were listed down quickly. No attention was given
to our explanations that we had no political involvement.
We were again made to lie face down, this time in an open
yard with our hands clasped in back of our necks. It was
quite chilly and my arms and legs were getting numb. I heard
a *carabinero* tell another that I was going to freeze. "Where
he is going," the second *carabinero* answered, "no clothes will
be needed."

I lay there from 12:30 until 8:00 p.m. We could relieve ourselves against a corner of the wall, but otherwise whenever one
of us dared to move an inch he was immediately beaten down
again. Then we were all taken to the stadium.

At the stadium our names were listed down again very quickly and we were taken to what we called cells. Actually these
were the locker rooms where the athletes changed clothes. At
the start there were forty-five of us in each of these small com-
partments. There were lines of people in the corridors and
they kept coming on and on all night from what we could
hear. So far we had been given no explanation of what they
intended to do with us, and no food had been distributed since

our arrest. There were Chileans and foreigners of different
ages, all of them arrested at home. There was a group of
functionaries of the Civil Registrar. They had been severely
beaten and one of them was in a bad way because he had a
stomach ulcer. He vomited all night long. Another one from
the El Teniente mine had been without food or water for three
whole days. We were all feeling very cold by then and we
found out that by lying close to each other back to back we
could get a little warmer.

The largest group among us, 90 percent I would say, were
factory workers. Their behavior was absolutely superb and
especially their sense of comradeship. When the inquiries were
held under torture they used to come out in groups singing
together and shaking their shirts over their heads with en-
couraging shouts to let us know that it was not so bad after
all. Their fighting tradition had made them the main target
of the Junta. Little by little, all foreigners who did not appear
to have any direct involvement with political activities in Chile
were placed in the same cell.

The Venezuelans, I think, were the most numerous, followed
by the Bolivians and Colombians. We were all thrown together
to prove, by our large number, that Allende had recruited
foreign leftists for very definite purposes.

This room where we were was built to accommodate 10 to
12 people but had 180 prisoners in it. We would take turns
sleeping. Those whose turn came could crouch down in the
middle of the room while the others stood up shoulder to shoulder or sat on the toilets or else on the wall which separated
them from the main part of the room. Sometimes we would
doze standing up, sort of leaning on each other. There was
no possibility of hygiene. The odor was unbearable. Our food
consisted of half a cup of bean soup and spaghetti once a
day or frequently just hot water with some salt and other
condiments. It was very hard to make those who had been
resting get up. Since the others would keep on talking to try
and stay awake, being totally exhausted, they had a hard
time falling asleep.

By the third or fourth night, around two or three in the
morning, we heard a strange noise. An officer seemed to be
screaming and swearing. The voice sounded completely hysterical. A truck had stopped a few minutes earlier by the stadium entrance, and we could guess that a large group of
people had arrived from the sound of beatings and the

screams. We heard someone say out loud that they were
coming from La Legua, a *población* where there had been
a lot of resistance. They were being beaten terribly. They were
told to yell their names and addresses quickly and then to
keep on running. From the sounds of beatings and the quick
steps we guessed that they were going through what we call
a "Polish corridor " (where you have to run between two files
of men who keep beating you). Other strange sounds made
clear to us that the new prisoners' heads were also being
beaten against the walls and doors. Then we heard shots and
inquiries as to whether they had just seen their comrades shot
to death. By the accents of the prisoners we could tell they
were from the *población*. This lasted for more than one hour —
between one and two o'clock in the morning. In our usually
noisy cell there was now a dead silence. Those who had been
sleeping were awake by now. We could hear our own breath-
ing and our hearts beating. Then there was the sound of water
being thrown from buckets and brooms sweeping around.

"They are washing away the blood," someone said.

From then on the uncertainty about what they intended to
do to us grew worse. A whole week went by. The new groups,
as they came in, were placed leaning on their hands against
the wall and were made to stay like that for several hours.
At that time there were about forty Brazilians in my cell. We
took our first bath after twenty days. There was an old
Bolivian with a heart condition who was quite sick. Two other
prisoners had ulcers and several others had fractured ribs.
After eight days we were questioned. This questioning was done
by *carabineros* in civilian clothes. The questions were very
superficial: Why had we come to Chile? What were our activities in the country and our relationship with other foreigners
and with Chileans? During these inquiries the prisoners were
beaten from time to time for no reason whatsoever. The group
that got the worst beating was the Dominicans. But none of
this was done systematically so we were not too frightened.
Another classification was made but it was very superficial,
separating those who were under suspicion from the others.
Only five or six of us were not suspected of anything. I found
myself among these. There were also some tourists and functionaries of international companies in this group. The bureau-
cratic work was so poorly coordinated that cards and even
files were lost. This created tremendous confusion.

We six Brazilians were thrown in with other groups of prisoners who should have been freed already. We now amounted
to around eight hundred people who could walk around in
the open area of the stadium. The other prisoners were by
then brought out into the open air once a day but they were
surrounded by machine guns while the cells were washed down.
This happened from the end of the first week on. Although
we were able to move around better in this larger room where
we found ourselves now, it was extremely cold because the
wind would blow in through the open doors and several of
the window panes were broken. The food was just as scarce
as ever and the sanitary conditions worse. The toilets were
out of order, the garbage accumulated in several corners and
the stench was unbearable. We could not wash ourselves since,
as I said before, we were only allowed to use the showers
after twenty days.

"The Chilean section of the International Red Cross distributed a few things — but very few. The Red Cross women
treated the prisoners very badly. When the prisoners' families
started sending packages they would open them and distribute
most of the food and cigarettes to the soldiers. It was terrible
when there was a delay in the distribution of our meager food
ration. We were simply starved. I will never forget those hungry faces as long as I live. We looked more like animals than
human beings. We would carefully save the peels of the few
oranges we received from time to time and eat them up slowly
throughout the day. Sometimes more compassionate soldiers
would throw us their loaves of bread.

There was practically no medical care. Many of us, due
to the cold and malnutrition were running the risk of pneu-
monia. They would then distribute some Vitamin C and aspirin.
Vitamin C on an empty stomach is murder!

One of my Brazilian comrades, Vanio Jose, died at the stadium. He had had gastric intestinal troubles. The nervous
tension which was our common lot made it worse. He got
no medical help. Three of the prisoners were doctors: a Brazilian, a Bolivian, and an Argentinian. They insisted that Vanio
should be taken to the hospital set up in the stadium. One
of the doctors accompanied Vanio, bringing a complete medical report they had written together. The report was torn up by
the army doctor, who said he was the only one there who
knew anything about medicine. Vanio Jose, by then, had rec-

tal vomiting. He had to undergo surgery immediately. Three days later he died. Those who saw his body said it bore marks of torture.

A whole month went by. Foreigners of several nationalities had been taken to the embassies of their countries. The Brazilians stayed on and so did the Bolivians, the Uruguayans, and those who came from the Caribbean — Haiti and the Dominican Republic. By that time we foreigners were called together and they read out a list describing each case. The great majority of us were to be thrown out of the country. Some had to be questioned again and others would be submitted to the judgment of the Military Junta. The officer in charge explained that those who were to leave the country had not been freed yet because there was no one responsible for them. Those who so wished could get in touch with the embassies of their countries through the representative of the Refugee Committee of the United Nations whom we would meet shortly. Before this first meeting took place all the Brazilians were called and placed in a circle. Two men started going around us with a sort of album with photographs and fingerprints comparing us to these. We noticed that the words on these papers were written in Portuguese. One of them spoke Spanish with a foreign accent. The other never said a word. By their appearance they could have been either Europeans or Americans.

A few days later a meeting was held with three people from the United Nations. They asked us to fill in papers indicating the countries of our preference. They explained that this concerned applications for political assylum and that they were trying to obtain temporary refuge from the Junta for those who intended to leave the country. Ten days later, members of the International Red Cross started visiting us with letters from our families. They gave us some assistance and the assurance that we were not to fear for our safety because the Junta had stated in answer to a request from the United Nations that the right of asylum would be respected. We said that many prisoners had undergone torture, but they said they had obtained no definite confirmation of this. Anyhow, at that moment they were mostly concerned with the problem of political asylum. By that time the Junta, probably because of international repercussions, was trying to create an appearance of justice and social order. In the meantime, groups of Chileans were being taken every day to a small field some distance from the stadium, used in normal times for bicycle races. Questionings were being held there with the use of electric shocks, beatings, and all sorts of threats. As for us, we received constant assurances that we would not be sent back to our country. At one point I was part of a group of Brazilians called in for questioning. We had machine guns pointed at us and were told to face the wall. Then they started taking us into the adjoining room two by two. When my turn came, I was questioned intensively concerning my activities in Chile and abroad. They were trying very hard to connect me with a Brazilian revolutionary organization to which I didn't belong. I was then told to wait outside while others were questioned. It was not long before I heard the sound of beatings and screams from the prisoners.

When they were through with all the others, they came to get me — the Chilean officer and the Brazilian in charge of the tortures, who was later identified by one of my *compañeros* as being Jose Alfredo Posck, an officer of the Centro de Informação de Marina (CENIMAR), which is connected with the CIA. I was taken to an isolated room quite a distance from there, with no *carabineros* within earshot.

The leaders of the Chilean group turned the light on and told Posck: "Now we want to see the techniques you people employ and how efficient they really are." They tied me on to the *pau de arara*, the "parrot's perch" — a horizontal pole from which a person is hung by hands and feet while being given shocks — which had already been set up near the electric-shock machine. By now the questions were being asked straight out in Portuguese. All the while I was given a series of shocks in the rectum and on the penis. The Chileans watched from close by. One of them looked at the torturer and remarked, "But they still don't talk!" They increased the voltage while threatening me: "So you seem determined to go back to Brazil? Won't it be nice to see again the dear old country? We came all the way out here just to take you back." I didn't utter a word and the Chilean officer appeared to be more disappointed all the time. This went on for two whole hours, and by then I was, of course, completely exhausted. When they put me down on the floor my body was shaking all over. This always happens after a long series of shocks, and there is no way to control it. It is an automatic reaction which was explained by Posck in technical terms.

I was then taken back to the room where the other Brazilians waited. I was kept away from them and we were not allowed to utter a word. When they were through with the whole thing one of the soldiers took me to a spot near the exit gate of the stadium, and I was kept there completely isolated from the other prisoners. It was night by then and I came to the conclusion that they intended to take me wherever I was going when no one would notice.

Early the next morning there was a redistribution of the prisoners and a change of the guard. The new soldier who took charge of me had not been informed of my special situation. When they announced over the loud speaker that all foreigners had to gather at a given spot I told the fellow that since I was a foreigner I had to join them, which he let me do.

The next day we were able to tell the representative of the International Red Cross and the member of the Refugee Committee what had happened. Four days later I was taken in for a medical examination by one of the Red Cross doctors who found on my body the marks of torture. He told me that a report had already been drawn and a protest sent to the Military Junta.

The Junta denied any presence or interference of the Brazilian police, stating that in special cases, whenever deemed necessary, Brazilian officials would be allowed to interrogate us in the presence of Chilean officers, but only concerning matters of interest to their government. They had also declared that in any event we would be freed.

Five days later I was part of the first foreign group to be taken to the refuge of Saint Francis Xavier under the protection of the Swiss flag.

MARIA AUXILIADORA BARCELLOS LARA

[Maria Auxiliadora Barcellos Lara is a Brazilian medical student and a political refugee. She was one of the seventy political prisoners released by the Brazilian government and flown out of the country in 1971 in exchange for the release of the Swiss ambassador who had been taken hostage by the Brazilian underground.]

The reception we were given by the Chilean people when we arrived from Brazil was unbelievable. I've never seen a people like them; so warm and with such a sense of solidarity. In the beginning — and this is what shocks me now — the Christian Democrats were the most open people; they had a kind of solidarity with the new government of Chile. They were people who at that point hadn't yet decided to join the fascists. So the reception was really incredible. The only restriction they placed on us in Chile was that we had to keep out of active participation in political activity. And we obeyed; that is, we didn't get involved in the Chilean parties. We followed Chilean politics, we knew about everything that was going on, but we couldn't take an active part in it. And we understood the government's position. One of the weapons the right wing used most against Allende was the accusation of foreign participation and the "denationalization of Chile." But, in fact, exactly the opposite was happening: this same right wing was receiving every imaginable kind of foreign aid — financial, moral, material, and political — to move against the Allende government. But the tactics they used were to blame

51

the violence on the government and to accuse foreigners of bringing arms to Chile and importing authoritarian ideologies, etc. In other words, the usual weapons, the lies that fascism uses to win over the masses. So, slowly but surely, the Christian Democrats, instead of growing more liberal, were turning toward the other side. Not so much because of economic problems, I think, as because of the constant ideological pressure and insecurity that was being created among the people. Especially among the small-scale manufacturers and merchants: the people who were most afraid of change but who had no idea of the dreadful consequences fascism would bring to Chile.

Well, in the university where I was a medical student (I studied for two and a half years in Chile) there was tremendous pressure, because doctors are one of the most reactionary sectors in Chile. You probably know about the participation of doctors in all the strike movements against government expenditures, etc. They are a stratum with that kind of aspiration; they want to move up the social ladder. And it's true that socialized medicine in Chile would have made it impossible for doctors to be more privileged, which I find fine. But they aspired to more. So there was tremendous pressure from the professors and from the administration. The first few months I thought of dropping out. I wasn't really doing anything politically; I had progressive friends, leftist friends and all that, but I wasn't involved myself. I could feel the increasing pressure against foreigners: they even boycotted us in classes. The right wing — the *momios* ["mummies"— slang for extreme right-wingers] — the professors and all the others treated us more or less like Jews. Any opportunity we had to take part in a seminar, to work in the operating room, to do anything, or hold any kind of commercial job, they'd make it impossible for us. I had nother friend at school. They arrested him. He was jailed in Chile under pressure from the right who kept saying that foreigners had weapons, that foreigners had contact with this or that party. But they had no evidence against him (he really hadn't done anything); he was a full-time student, studying at the psychiatric hospital. In other words, about eighteen hours of his day were accounted for, so it was ridiculous to try to prove anything against him. But that gave us an idea of the kind of pressure the government was getting from the sectors on the right. This was in August 1972. They only held him for a week. After that he returned to his normal routine of study, etc.

Well, the pressure against foreigners in Chile was mounting daily. They even held demonstrations against us. Sometimes I'd be walking along and hysterical people would say to me, "Why don't you get out of Chile, guerrillas; we don't want you here, etc., etc." Just because we were speaking Portuguese. In other words, more and more people were feeling it (even tourists who were just visiting); everybody felt the change in atmosphere.

When the coup took place, tons of tourists were arrested, people who had nothing to do with anything. And I know of at least three of them who are still being held (October 11 they will have been in jail one month); they had passports, all their identification was in order, they were spending a month, or in some cases twenty-one days, in Chile and then returning to Brazil. They had their return tickets and everything. All their money was taken, all their identification, everything they had. They were left with no recourse, no identification, nothing.

As far as we were concerned, we were living in the center of the city. When the coup took place they labeled the area a "Traffic Prohibited Zone." In other words, if you wanted to go out you had to have special permission from the military command. On the morning of September 11 I was in my house. I was getting ready to go out when a friend came by to tell us what was going on. In the beginning we just waited to see what would happen, because it could have turned out to be just another unsuccessful coup like on June 29, which was a temporary thing. (I lived through that, too; I was living two blocks from La Moneda, so I saw the tanks, the shootouts in the streets and everything. It was just about the same time, nine o'clock in the morning, when I was on my way to school.) So we decided to wait and see. There were people staying with us who had nothing to do with what was going on, who weren't political exiles or anything, so we sent them somewhere else and stayed in the house by ourselves.

Well, what happened in Chile is that there really were only the *momios* and the left. So every neighbor was either a potential ally or a potential enemy. We had neighbors who were in the state intelligence service. It was a very shaky situation.

The people in the building knew our circumstances, that we were political exiles, and so on. We spent two days in the house. We even slept in the cellar one night because we had heard from friends, by phone, that other friends of ours who lived in various parts of the city had been arrested. So we decided to sleep in the basement. There were a lot of people who weren't on the left or anything, but who were friendly to us, and they helped us a lot.

On Thursday, September 13, we were at my house and we went out at great risk, because we were in a maximum security zone. We could hear shooting the whole night. It so happens that the Tacna Regiment (one of the most important regiments in Santiago), the officer training school, and the school for new recruits were all on my corner. So there was an incredible amount of shooting. We weren't sure if it was just meant to scare people. Some sounded like executions because there would be three or four shots, and then silence. This went on for two whole days.

Our neighbors who had sympathies with the left were scared to death. Many of their friends and relatives had been arrested. Afterwards I went to the house of some Chilean friends, people from school who were not leftists themselves but were with us all the same. They were hoping that as a result of the campaign against a civil war and the pacification campaign staged by the right, there would be a greater respect for human life. They would always tell me, "The Communists have no respect for life, but the right does." But I would say, "Those principles are going to crumble; they have nothing to do with the politics we're going to see in Chile now. In Chile now, society either moves forward or it moves backward; There's no third possibility." Well, these same friends took me and three other friends to the Mexican Embassy. We stayed there until we left for Mexico.

I'd rather not give any names, but I have definite information that three women I know were raped. They were raped in their own houses. The day of the coup I tried to get in touch by phone with the greatest possible number of my friends. They told me that one of them had been arrested. He was held for about four hours and then released. Later, he was hiding in the house of another friend when his problems ended. He was killed. This is definitely true, because I heard it from somebody who was in Brazil, who traveled to Brazil from Chile. He was a worker who had a job in one of the industrial belts. He'd been in Chile for a year. I don't know how he died.

I reached another friend, a woman, by phone. She was surrounded in the slum where she lived and told me the slum was being bombed and that they needed help. Could I, she asked, give medical assistance? A lot of people had been wounded and there was no way for them to get out. She said the best they could do was resist to the end, that they had no other choice. But I couldn't move either because we were under curfew and it was impossible to get around through the city.

Of the three friends of mine who were raped, none of them would say so. They were so afraid of revealing their situation over the phone that they didn't tell me until three days later. Over the phone they would only say, "Yes, everything's fine." They didn't say what had happened because they were afraid the military would come back. The soldiers had taken their money, their identification, everything they had.

THREE VENEZUELANS

[The three Venezuelan revolutionists who gave this testimony were all in Chile working and studying, after being forced to leave Venezuela as the result of their involvement in armed-struggle organizations there.]

The building where I lived was about a block from La Moneda Palace, where Allende was. The morning of the coup we tried to leave the building, but since we lived so close to La Moneda it was literally taken by the army and the *carabineros,* so it was impossible for us to go out into the street, and we had no choice but to remain inside. At about 6:00 p.m. a commission of women from the National Party, who were engaged in internal vigilance inside the building, called us — at least they asked me for my papers. My papers were in order. The one who vouched for me as a serious person not involved in politics was the person who rented the apartment to me, and because of that the commission left me alone. Now two guys from the Dominican Republic who lived there, Gilberto and Ricardo, were arrested that same night. Without a doubt these *compañeros* were held for the plain and simple reason that they were Black.

If before in Chile it was a virtue to be Black because there are hardly any colored people there, recently it changed into a nightmare. People of color who walked in the streets were virtually lynched. Someone saw a Black man being lynched. Another Venezuelan *compañero,* also Black, went out of his house to go to the Venezuelan Embassy and in the two blocks he walked he was stopped twice, and in those two times he lost about two hours because they separated him from the whites, stood him against the wall, and shot at him when he tried to catch a taxi.

So, we saw that there was a special thing against foreigners, against Blacks. Black was synonymous with Cuban. There was the case where they grabbed Zulueta, a Black, and a white man together. Then they took them to a commissariat of *carabineros*. When they arrived there, the person in charge was annoyed at the *carabineros* and said: "You aren't supposed to bring these people here alive. Why do you bother to bring these people here alive? These people you should kill where you grab them." Then they forced them down on the floor and simply because of his color, they kicked and beat the Black guy until they were tired. Since the other had no problems, he began to explain that they were students. They showed their passports, but the *caribineros* didn't care about that. They kicked only the Black guy; they didn't touch the other one.

There is another very important thing. Scenes of horror were witnessed in the central part of town because a communique announced that at 11:00 sharp the air force was going to bomb La Moneda. Allende had said earlier that he was not going to step down. And at 11:00 or ten to 11:00 the men who were guarding our building went to all the apartments and told everyone to go down to the basement because the bombs might miss and fall on the building, since it was scarcely a block away from La Moneda. The people were very worried, quite horrified. There were scenes of weeping, shouting, hysteria, and at just about 11:00 the air force began bombing. The windows of the building, the doors and windows of the apartments were broken by the impact of a plane which passed precisely overhead and dropped rockets on La Moneda.

We spent almost two pretty tough days there. The firing was continual. Day and night it was exactly the same, and the worst was that after a couple of days you couldn't believe that it was just among the military and not a civilian resistance. Then the shots were so close together, so continuous, that you couldn't believe that it was a civilian type of resistance. It had to be a problem among the military, since you could distinguish all kinds of arms. They were using as many heavy arms as light arms, and they used tanks, bazookas, mortars, all those kinds of weapons which only the military has. There the area was practically surrounded and beseiged; you couldn't enter or leave.

Two days later they called a kind of truce and the people who didn't live inside that sector were allowed to leave. Because of the abnormal situation of the coup, people had had to remain in offices or in buildings where friends lived. We took advantage of this opportunity to leave that area, since after a certain length of time it would be cordoned off again and you wouldn't be able to enter or leave. It was quite a combat zone since it was there where the snipers were. The military answered the snipers with all the weapons they had — there was no discrimination of any kind. So the best thing was to get out of the area.

We left on foot until we got beyond the Plaza Italia, which is in the rich neighborhoods where the people with economic resources live. It was like leaving the world of nightmare for the world of happiness, because there the people were walking around calmly eating ice cream, buying stuff on the street, just as if nothing had happened. Now, it's important to point out this behavior as showing how fascism is the expression of a class at a given moment which they need in order to recuperate their riches. While La Moneda was being bombed, while the snipers were being killed, while there was a horrible cross-fire, Chilean television was showing its normal programs, and at that moment you could see the soap operas, Walt Disney cartoons, as if in this country there was absolutely nothing happening.

A woman who lived opposite the National Stadium told us that she could see a lot of army trucks parked there at the stadium door, and she could see how they took out the corpses wrapped in blue sheets and carried them to the trucks. The trucks were so full that the bodies they threw on top would fall to the ground and they would have to pick them up and throw them back on. In other words, there was an extraordinary massacre there.

I also heard from a person who saw the banks of the Mapocho River, which virtually crosses the city of Santiago. He could see hundreds of corpses, among which were the bodies of many Black people.

ANTONIO HERNANDEZ

[Antonio Hernández is a Colombian who belonged to a revolutionary organization in his own country. When the government began to prosecute members of his organization he fled to Chile as a political refugee.]

About a year before the coup, a civilian rightist commando group beat me up and tried to interrogate me. We did not know if they were part of the Patria y Libertad party or some other group, but we were sure it must have had something to do with *Investigaciones*. This is an organization of civil "investigations" which functioned and still functions in Chile.

It happened at a time when they were searching the houses of various foreigners. I was walking near the Plaza Italia when they picked me up in a civilian car—a small van. I do not remember if there were five or six guys. I immediately identified them as being from *Investigaciones* so that when they told me to go with them I didn't resist at all. Nor did I try to escape. In a wooded park near the Plaza Italia they took me out and began to punch me. They hit me and asked me a series of questions about the revolutionary movement in Colombia, which they, if course, identified me with, and about how I had gotten to Chile, things that had to do with entry and exit of Latin American exiles. Later, they just left me lying there since I was quite badly beaten up. I don't know how long I stayed there like that. When I came to and remembered what had happened, I simply got up and went home. Later I had to get medical treatment at the Central Clinic. We decided not to report this to the police because we

didn't know if the group was from the police itself or some
rightist organization. I discussed it with a group of friends
and we came to the conclusion it was a rightist commando
group.

At that time I happened to talk to several Chilean *compañeros* who had seen tortures in the countryside. These tortures were not carried out by the armed forces but rather by
civilians, sort of "White Guards." According to them, in one
case a group of armed civilians got hold of several peasants,
tortured them, bound them with barbed wire, and left them in
the countryside. This case was publicized later in a leftist newspaper but no one paid any attention to it, not even the government authorities, and least of all the Chilean Justice Department. Well, this has something to do, more or less, with the
forms of torture that were used after the coup, and the way
in which they went about preparing the coup. It showed that
the preparation of the coup was not just spur of the moment,
as some military men of Chile would like to have it appear
now.

Another illustration of this was given to me by a friend,
a Chilean worker who lived in the *población* of Lo Hermida,
and who saw the repression against that *población*. Other
compañeros, who I'm sure I can trust, have also told me
how that *población* was repressed and tortured. My friend
had a relative who is or was active in the Patria y Libertad
party, and during the six months prior to the coup he kept
telling my friend to leave the *población*. He knew my friend
was on the left—if not an active militant of any party at least
a sympathizer of the UP. He advised him to get out of there—
the sooner the better—or at least to leave at the first sign of
a coup. My friend took this warning seriously because it was
from his relative. We both deduced, therefore, that the objective of the right, both military and civilian, was to have a
strong coup, and that the right might also have some plans
that would surpass the coup itself.

Another thing which shows the preparation of the coup was
the attempted coup of June 29—the *tancazo*—which was also
preceded by a series of detentions in the *poblaciones*. I also
learned about this from a friend who lived in the *población*.
Later, after this attempted coup, a film about it by a now dead
Argentine journalist was being shown in the area. The Military Investigation Department or the Military Justice Department, which was making an investigation of the attempted

coup, forbade it. They were especially interested in erasing all traces of the *tancazo*.

Then they put the famous "arms control" law into effect in a very visible way. I happened to see them search a factory near where I was working. They humiliated the workers, calling them communists, sons of bitches, a series of insults to offend them, trying to provoke them. They made the workers put their hands behind their backs, bound them, and made them stand against the wall as if they were going to shoot them, while they "requisitioned" equipment— I happened to witness the destruction of the machinery. This operation was a direct part of the preparation for the coup. It wasn't just a search for arms. They only searched visible places — for example, inside the machinery, inside desks. If someone wanted to hide a revolver or rifle, they certainly wouldn't leave it there. While one of the intentions was to physically disarm the people, the main objective was to disarm them psychologically so that the coup could be carried out as it was.

During the days before the coup, I remember that a group of us — Colombians, other Latin Americans, and Chileans — were all waiting for a coup at any moment. Indeed we'd talk ironically when making appointments for the next day — "if the coup doesn't. . ." If we were going to the doctor, we'd say, "if there's no coup."

On the day of the coup a committee of the right-wing National Party took over almost the whole street I lived on and assumed a menacing attitude toward several foreigners who lived there. I don't know why they didn't report us. Instead, on the first night of the coup they shot at our apartment, and also at the house of a Chilean woman who had practically nothing to do with politics but who had shown solidarity with the foreigners who were living there. After the shooting at our house, there was no further harassment. Instead, most of the people in the apartments began to show their desire to collaborate with us, to give us any help we needed to get out of there. They managed to get us out of there in the end, which was difficult since people were not going into the street right then.

We couldn't go to friends' houses since most were in trouble themselves, being foreigners or Chileans who had something to do with the socializing process in Chile by the UP. So instead we decided to go to the Mexican Embassy.

ROBERTO

[Roberto is a militant in the Socialist Party of Chile. At the time of the coup he was working as a director of the SP's radio station. He is thirty years old, married, and has children. Roberto was given asylum in the Mexican Embassy.]

The night before the coup I was meeting with a top leader of the Socialist Party. We received a call from one of the leftist radio stations informing us that one of their contacts inside the armed forces had said that the situation was rather confused. Many officials had advised their families not to go into the center of the city on the following day, and the brother of Colonel Supper (who headed the attempted coup of June 29), who is an ex-military official of Patria y Libertad in Concepción, had traveled to Santiago two days prior and was up to something. We began to check this information through different channels. Unfortunately, the contact who gave us this information was an officer of low rank. We tried, therefore, to confirm it with someone of higher rank. But it was incredible — we ran head-on into a wall of treason. All those who had always shown themselves to be very good friends, with whom we had meetings, and with whom we discussed rather important details of the armed forces, told us that there was nothing to worry about, that we should go to sleep — all of our great contacts, including some generals.

Around 2:00 a.m. we went to sleep. At 7:00 a.m. this same Socialist Party leader called and told me to go to Radio Corporación, the SP's station, because the fascist movement by the military was coming, that it had actually already begun. So we went directly to the station, and when we arrived there we realized that the very same high military officials who had told us not to worry were heading the coup or supporting its leaders. The treason was clearly evident.

The political leader who called me had been in contact since early morning with President Allende. In Radio Corporación there was a direct telephone hook-up to the president's office, and he spoke constantly with him. Let me make something clear — the president always said that he didn't know if it was a movement of the entire armed forces or was simply being done by the navy in Valparaíso. I understand this to mean that the president did not want there to be a great massacre, because contrary to what the fascists said, the people were not preparing against a coup. There was no "Plan Z" or anything like that — that was a crude self-serving fabrication by the fascists.

Around 8:30 a.m. we knew for sure that it was the armed forces who were conducting this show. So the political director, together with other officials of the radio station, began to call upon the people to mobilize. President Allende spoke once or twice on the radio, utilizing our hook-up, but between 9:00 and 10:00 a.m. the transmission plant was being bombed and the frequencies were cut off. This also shows how the fascists lied in saying that the left was prepared for a coup, that it had a "Plan Z" to kill all the soldiers, etc. If we had been preparing ourselves for a coup we would have had emergency equipment ready the moment our power was cut off, but we had nothing like that.

We stayed and listened to what was going on in the president's office over the microphone. We conversed with him or with his aide to find out what was happening inside and what we could do from outside. Although our transmitting plant was bombed, we had electronic equipment inside that allowed us to transmit on FM and short wave. So we formed a pool of people and called up different industries to tell them what wavelengths we would broadcast on. Every half-hour we broadcast for five minutes: the political director spoke in the name of the Socialist Party and called on the workers to organize themselves for the struggle and told how the resistance should be oriented. The technicians explained that we could broadcast only five minutes every half hour so that the military would not be able to locate where we were broadcasting from. This transmission was maintained until around 4:30 in the afternoon, when the political director said that it was insane to stay inside because the radio station would obviously be visited by the military and there would be blood and fire.

At around 10:00 a.m. a small portable transmitter had been taken from the transmitting plant so it could be put in a vehicle and transmit from outside. The people who tried to leave with this equipment found themselves facing a .30-caliber machine gun nest which let off a round of fire when they went out, placing the *compañeros* in grave danger in returning to their posts.

We kept in contact with President Allende until approximately 2:00 p.m. At this time the person in the president's office who was attending the microphone said that everything was very difficult and that we shouldn't call because they could not distract anyone in order to answer. He left the microphone on, however, on top of a table, so we could continue hearing what went on inside. We recorded this and the tape is now outside Chile. There were more than eighteen of us inside the station and we heard how the president gave orders to fight and resist, how they took out cases of munitions, how they gave out some arms (which belonged to the palace guard and had all been there before), and later we heard a long silence. After ten minutes of profound silence we heard intense firing, and later a new silence. No more than three or five minutes passed when we heard the voices of military officials saying, "Lieutenant, here is a case; give me something to open this desk with," but not once did they speak about President Allende. Later we learned that the junta was saying that the president had committed suicide in his office. We were listening to everything that went on inside his office and at no time did they speak about President Allende. This, of course, is very curious and makes us imagine a series of things with respect to the way the president died.

Later, at 4:30 p.m. we tried to leave through a hole we made in the back of the station (we were on the second floor). We tried to go toward the Banco del Estado. When we were leaving a soldier threw a grenade from the bank's terrace. Fortunately, it was a nine-second grenade and the soldier must have counted very slowly because it went off in midair and did not hurt us. We went back to the station and at around 5:00 p.m. we left through the main door. We surprised the military patrol outside because they thought everything was under control. When they saw eighteen people leave they came at us with their guns ready, threw us to the ground, and searched us completely, without asking for any identification. Later they told us to go toward the Banco del Estado through a passage that is there. Half way through the passage another patrol made us stand against the wall and again searched us completely. They told us to continue toward the Banco del Estado. At the door of the bank another patrol stopped and searched us. Later they made us enter the bank where there were some four or five hundred people detained. But already the conversation with the military, in spite of being nervous, was somewhat friendly. The people there were working on the military psychologically so that they would let everyone leave. This conversation had results because one of the commanders of the group said, "Okay, the men on one line, the women on another, you are going to leave. You have to be quick because at 6:00 p.m. there is a curfew." We were on the line when someone recognized the political director, and the commander arrested him. When we left we heard shots being fired from all over. It was the high point of the resistance. Later we were able to verify that the Junta was lying since they said that this director had given himself up voluntarily. He may have been somewhat disguised, but in spite of that they recognized him and arrested him — he didn't give himself up.

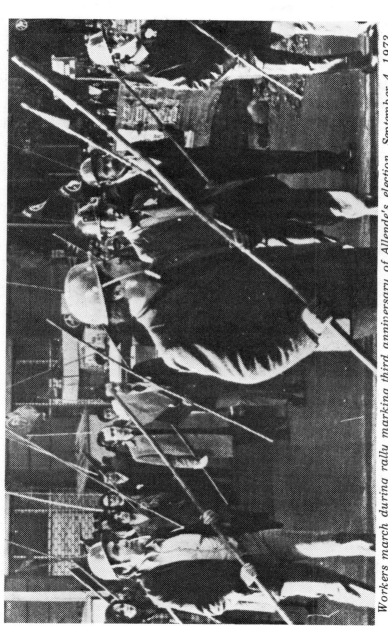

Workers march during rally marking third anniversary of Allende's election, September 4, 1973.

La Moneda, the presidential palace, September 11, 1973.

Leftist literature heads for the bonfire.

Above: Political prisoners at Pisagua camp in northern Chile.

Right: Under guard at the National Stadium.

ANA MARIA

[Ana María is a young Chilean militant of the Communist Party. She was working as a functionary of the party at the time of the coup.]

What did we feel just before the coup?

Well, we Chileans had a chance to get sort of a preview in the *tancazo;* and we reacted by simply working harder each day, with more fortitude, forever holding out more hope, but also knowing that the work was futile. We knew that much of what we did was in vain, that it took us nowhere, that we were part of the pattern of this horrible wasted jumble of marches, of women walking through the center of the city on our way to UNCTAD — the place built to hold the UN Conference on Trade and Development in 1972, which then became the center for all sorts of political and cultural activity for the left — on our way to see General Prats, the loyal head of the armed forces, to send flowers to his wife, or on our way to the Ministry of Defense because our Señor Prats happened to be busy at the moment, and then finding we couldn't get into the Ministry of Defense anyway. We were organizing public demonstrations, moving people around, but knowing deep down that it was fruitless and in vain. We were aware of what might happen at any moment, but on we marched, and we still continued sending flowers to General Prats's wife.

That's how we are, we Chileans. The peaceful road, our famous road. Where did it lead us?

It is awful remembering those things. We loved Allende. We were able to hear much of what he said the last day. We could sense what he was about to do when he called to us over Radio Magallanes, giving us by that act (with what many

75

call vanity) some clue of what we had to do. But what were we doing? We were only a huge mass of people believing in something that changed from one day to the next, in spite of our total awareness of the situation. But one never knows when such things will happen, and then it all falls to pieces in a minute. And that is how Allende by his own example was giving us a path to follow. "Come to my defense at La Moneda," he said at one point. But later he said, "Don't come." What does a person do at that moment? When some two hours before everything was as it had always been; and then all at once you see all this heavy artillery, and all these planes flying over La Moneda, the whole horrible sequence of events. And then we stood with our hands in our pockets, crying over the "Chilean road," lamenting it all, and dearly loving our *compañero* Allende. What can a people without guns do? What can a people who believed in nonviolence do? Run away? Flee? That's right — just like me. Many have found asylum, as I have. All of us are a people that have fled.

How do you face a tank with a hand gun? How do you face a horde of reddened faces — those soldiers with their guns trained on you, those machine guns that can kill all of you in a single burst? So you kill a few yourself, but what do you gain? You kill a few, but there are a thousand behind them. They multiply. What can you do? They swarm over and smother you. Nothing is important anymore; even if one lives life just a little, by some instinct, by some normal instinct, but not even that is very important. So what do you do? Do you fight or not fight? Fight and be damned. Refuse to fight and be damned. What do you do? You stay around until the cannons or the tanks come down on you. Or one of the soldiers comes at you with one of those things; or they enter your house and ransack everything, respecting no one, not even the old women. And there you are, right in the middle, chewing out your insides, and hoping and waiting for a Chilean army of your own to spring into existence to fight back. And it is all a utopian dream, it really is. So there you stay, unable to do anything. There you stay, impotent, like a lump of shit, wishing to go back so that you could do something. But what do you do, what do I do? Nothing. . .

We used to watch the political situation — and we knew about the generals, we followed every footstep that each of them took. But we had to go along and play the game with them. That was our position. I am no expert at these things, but, yes, I can say that I worked hard at it. Our weeks were filled with rushing around — from work to the political meetings, where you heard the report, which of course upset you. The whole mass of workers were upset, they didn't like it. They were aware that something was about to happen and they were asking for arms; but our fucking "Chilean road" kept us from facing up to it all, and from demanding more strenuously what we needed. The people were aware all along of what was happening.

As for our work — it was barren. We knew that our industries weren't running well. Okay, so they were being nationalized. And then there was our voluntary labor. We knew voluntary labor would not help the country in the least at that moment. We knew about the robbery and stealing that was going on inside those factories by the very same workers; we knew about so many irregularities. We were brimming over with them. But we continued to go on to the volunteer jobs. "Let's go pitch in with some voluntary work!" That's where we were.

The political caucusing, that too is where we were at. But we did not know where it would all end. We had no idea!

Like the other day when you had to be up early to stand watch, or when you stayed all night in your place of work because of the situation. That is where you would find us; we were always standing by. But we knew it wouldn't help.

Then came the moment of real confrontation, and our organization didn't budge. We didn't know how to get communications going in spite of all our security measures. Despite our knowing the gravity of the situation, we had no point of contact because the *compañeros* had all been rounded up. And so it was that the steps that we had to take had already been blocked. We knew previously that the phones were tapped. We were not organized. The machinery did not work. At least that is what happened where I was. I can't speak of anywhere else without being unjust.

When I served in the Communist Party I had several functions; within my cell I was organization secretary, and later on propaganda secretary. In the local committee at work I became part of the Commission on Education.

As a member of the commission my job was to educate the new members of our party. To do that it was necessary to work to find good teachers who could give classes that would bring the message to everyone in straightforward language, to bring all the members up to a certain level of political education. That, in itself, consumed a great deal of our time; it would not be a lie to say that what we lacked most was time to do all these things.

Next, as the primary duty of a militant, came the voluntary work in which we would participate every weekend. Before the coup the most important work was the spring planting. Every member could see how important that was.

Then there were the rightists with their *miguelitos,* which we had to clear away. *Miguelitos* are like bent nails that have both points sticking up so that when they are scattered on a well-traveled road they puncture tires and stop traffic. We've had lots of experience with *miguelitos* in the past months, forming work parties to get the *miguelitos* off the road so that the vehicles could pass.

With the truck owners who went out on "strike," their vehicles were not confiscated. On the contrary. The truck owners supported by Vilarín, head of the owners' federation, and by the doctors and businessmen were given even more trucks. It was one of those government policies that we disagreed with. We thought that these new vehicles should be handed over to MOPARE, the group of independent truckers who supported the UP, because they were the ones who really were working. They were the ones who actually picked up the flour from the loading docks and brought it into the center of the cities. But the party was against any confiscation of those trucks.

It was obvious that with all of those people against us, something had to be done, something with force behind it, so that once and for all the right might realize that we, too, had some power, and that we, too, could do something.

In October 1972 the party said that it would be good to let the merchants remain independent if they so wished. The party said that it was necessary for the merchants to be left alone, because they, too, were a part of the people and had a right to live. That was the party's opinion when the "public food basket" program was being elaborated. And, well, many *compañeros* asked that it please, please follow through with the idea of the public food basket, and not let the merchants have those distribution rights; that it be done directly via the people, that the people distribute directly from the factory to the populace. Unfortunately, it was not done at that time. It was only done much later. It would have been an excellent way to provide for everyone, with everyone having his or her own food basket.

When the party realized this, already it was a little late. Never was a thing done straight off, we never did things at the opportune moment, when it was being asked for, when we all needed it. We were all hungry and we needed an adequate distribution system so that everyone would receive the same. We needed to stop the boycott by the right, which always did what suited its fancy, and today does what it wishes. That is what should have been done, *compañeros.*

The *tancazo* came in June and from June to September the coup was being planned in earnest. Everyone in Chile knew that the coup was coming, and that it was necessary to prepare ourselves.

There were certain security measures which were not, let us say, known to us, since we were only rank and filers. That is why I could not say how the preparations were made. I do know that the Fourteenth Party Congress was coming up, in which they would discuss all the different positions. There was a lot of debate at meetings because we were asking for some kind of direct action. We asked for guns, we fought to get guns. But this Fourteenth Congress was not held; even with all that security we never had a chance to hold it.

No member of the party had a right to Sundays off. You didn't even complain about it. I did once in a special situation when I was near collapse. But to me a good militant should dedicate himself completely to his party. Certainly, we worked on Sundays. It made sense, for there was a great deal to do, a lot of work, very little time, hardly any socializing, one hardly stopped to eat. When you could drag yourself away, you found a corner to sleep in for a bit, which was the best thing you could do. Or maybe you could read a little something, but that was it.

In political work and in our official duties everything was very intense, and every day we were battling with some *momio* who stood in the way. When it was time to get chummy with the Christian Democrats, well, there we were, although we didn't like very much surrendering to a Christian Democrat. It all meshed together during the working hours.

Later in the day came work which we were especially dedicated to, and that took away our afternoons and evenings too. And so it often went the same way into the weekends. On Saturday and Sunday we had volunteer work to do. We were given a certain place to go to harvest corn, plant potatoes, to do so many things. There were so many agricultural jobs to be done. Or if it wasn't in agriculture, then in our own place of work.

Chile is an exception among most Latin American countries in that its armed forces have stayed on the side of the government. We thought that this time it would be the same. But you can see for yourselves. Sure, we knew that there were problems, and grave problems. We knew that there was a center of insurgency. We knew how many we could count on, who was with us and who was not. But we had believed their endless boasting about that iron discipline, etc., etc. We had confidence in that Chilean military spirit. We always had a little hope. That is why we thought that the military establishment might one day turn about. And that's where our most important task lay, because they could possibly turn to be on our side. And so that is what we had to do, we had to turn them to come to our aid. You see, they had the guns, and they did not come around to our side; but we used to think that that institution could at any given moment come to the aid of the government, just as it had in suppressing the *tancazo.*

In the last days before the coup, we were bored, we were fed up with political tasks. We were tired of kissing General Prat's ass. We were sick and tired of being playmates for the Christian Democrats while they laughed at us, and while they pontificated about the Constitution and called the government unconstitutional. It was all a worn-out deception.

And me personally? For me, if something was going to happen, well, then it happened; because you couldn't take it any more, and no one could fight it after so many years of being in the movement. We were exhausted, I mean really wiped out. Fatigue like that was not so much physical as it was mental. We were wishing that whatever was going to break loose would just do so. We were at the end of our rope. That was the feeling that you got. You could feel it in the lines for cigarettes and in the bread lines. By then there was no more bread. The people were saying, "All right, bring on the civil war, but at least let us have bread." Or they would say, "Let the war come but let us have cigarettes." That was one of the greatest struggles within the party. "NO CIVIL WAR!" It was one of the things we had fought against all our lives. "NO CIVIL WAR!" That rallying cry had lost its popularity, and not even we knew what we wanted. It was a very strange state of mind. As I said, I personally would have preferred that something break wide open. No, not just to have a piece of bread, but to stop that overwhelming tiredness that had come over us.

At such times you would say to yourself, "All right, I am a part of it all, but there are those higher up, there are people managing all this, who should use a heavy hand," as we had shouted out in front of the Congress. Without knowing exactly how the party felt after the attempted takeover in June, I personally shouted at the president, "Use a heavy hand and close down the Congress!" And the president said to us, "No, no, the Congress will not be closed. Let us follow the Chilean road. Let us continue."

Thus it was that in those days before the coup, I was wishing with all my heart that something would just break loose. You couldn't take it any more. And the people on the right wanted it too, because they missed their piece of bread, and their cigarettes, and their food at the table, too. As you all know, the right moves first to conquer the middle class, because the middle class controls everything and they don't want to let go. The lack of bread and cigarettes was a way of wearing the people down, and the middle class was asking for their own. Sure, they were right, but, you say to yourself, "How pitiful. How pitiful I am in spirit. How sad a human being is when in the end the struggle is for a piece of bread, or a cigarette, for a plate of food." But that's how it is.

Chile is my country as it was before the coup — the country as it is today does not resemble Chile. With that, I'll tell you what I think of Chile. What can I say about the notorious rivers of blood that are flowing? What is there to say? That I don't recognize my country? *That* is not Chile. No, it cannot be. Chile is our *compañeros* who are in jail, in the National Stadium, who are held on the island prisons. Chile is university rectors who are in prison suffering from exposure in freezing temperatures. Today Chile is nothing but a prison.

JUAREZ FERRAZ DE MAIA

[Juarez Ferraz de Maia is a twenty-six year-old Brazilian high-school teacher and a political refugee.]

I'm from the Brazilian state of Goiás, an agricultural region where the large landowners exploit the cheap labor of the peasants and farmers and where the white slave trade flourishes. It could be said that the region is in the feudalistic stage of Brazil's capitalist development. My family were peasants in this area and we were very poor.

After the Brazilian coup of 1964, which overthrew the constitutional President João Goulart, I began to participate in a Christian movement that was defending national interests. For example, we denounced Mr. Selling, an American who had bought up about one million square kilometers of land, the entire region of Goiás in Amazonia, in addition to the state of Pará. He owned almost one-eighth of the national territory. This made me ask myself it this threatens Brazilian territorial integrity or not. And I would ask the North American citizens if they would like a Brazilian to buy an eighth of the North American territory. So we conducted campaigns against the North American land purchases in the states of Goiás, Maranhão and Amazonia.

Not long after that we were arrested, imprisoned, and subjected to the "democratic" methods of interrogation. For example, I was tortured in the federal police building of Goiás. This was already in 1967. We did not yet have an organized resistance. At that time I saw *compañera* Annette and her two sons — eight and ten years old — violently tortured near me. She participated in the Christian movement called Popular Action. I cannot forget her screams from the electric shocks in her vagina, in her sexual organs. Here I would like to ask the North American people if they really agree with the policies conducted in Brazil by the United States' best known repressive institutions — like the CIA and various institutions which take special care of the situation in Latin America, take care of us, for example.

I eventually obtained amnesty from the military government of Costa e Silva, with the help of the Masons, and left prison. The Masons are a big movement in Brazil and my father is a member. After that I was elected president of the state student federation by an absolute majority of the students of the state of Goiás. From that moment we began a national campaign in defense of national rights and against the dictatorial policies of the military government, against the economic, political, and social aggression of foreign capitalism, which did not represent our interests. From that time on, I was taken prisoner a total of thirty-nine times — I was even taken prisoner once when there was a demonstration in the United States.

In 1969 I was condemned by a military tribunal and I had to go underground. Why go into hiding? I would like to explain this very clearly to the North American citizens, who might say, "Look, he went underground because the guy is an international communist." I would prefer to go to jail and suffer torture than to be underground, because to be in hiding means to be a stranger in your own country. You are outside your own world, like a fish out of water. I went underground not to run away, but to fight. So I did not abandon what I believed. I continued to struggle but in a different manner. This particular way meant that you had to leave everything — the university, your *compañeros,* friends, home town, the things you had most loved. My name then appeared in newspapers every day as a terrorist, wanted by the police, and as such, a dangerous element. I was underground for two years, from 1969 to 1971.

Finally in April 1971, because of the worsening of an illness I had contracted in prison, I left the country clandestinely and went to Uruguay. There I asked for and received asylum in Chile.

I came to Chile in April 1971 as an exile from Brazil. I joined the ranks of the Chilean people and worked in a furniture factory which had been intervened by the state. I was also taking courses at the Catholic University. I thus became an integral part of the Chilean reality, participating in the life of workers, students, and the Chilean people. The affection and support shown for us and all the Latin American refugees in that country was really a heartwarming thing. We could never forget the Chilean people's faith and affection, particularly on the part of the average citizen, the poor people, workers, and students.

But the bourgeoisie, the people who were connected with North American and international capitalists, saw the political refugees as human monsters and waged a direct campaign against them as soon as they arrived. This persecution was not official, but was manifest in the streets, in the clubs, as if we were Jews in Germany during the time of Hitler. It was that way for the Argentines, Peruvians, and Bolivians. The Chilean bourgeoisie has a particular racial prejudice against the Bolivians who have always lived there; they were the most outcast.

The bourgeoisie eventually began a systematic campaign against the refugees in Chile. But we did not worry about it because it came directly from the Chilean bourgeoisie and we were not part of that society. We were part of the Chilean people— the people who were producing, the people who had professions — not the idle.

From the time I arrived in April 1971 until June 29, 1973, when the first attempted coup took place, there was a seriously institutionalized opposition to the constitutional government of Salvador Allende. The Chilean fascists began to publish things against foreigners in Chilean newspapers like *La Segunda*. Before the coup, a student *compañero* (who was not an exile or a refugee, but simply an architecture student) was stoned by some women in the streets of Providencia, a wealthy section of Santiago, just because he was Black. One no longer felt secure or free to walk the streets, to converse in your own language, or to have an accent that was not Chilean, because you were then singled out and branded. An interesting thing happened to me and another Brazilian *compañero* about a month before the coup. We were in a bar when a guy heard us speaking Portuguese and began to say talk about how the foreigners were coming to Chile to massacre the Chilean people, to rob the Chilean people, how we were terrorists, how we had to leave the country, and how Chile, having the luck to be the only country in Latin America which had no Blacks, today was suffering the disgrace of having Blacks walking the streets. Given the circumstances, we paid and left the bar. Things like that were happening every day, even in buses. In Providencia especially there were concrete aggressions against Brazilians and Panamanians because they were Black, and against Bolivians who were the poorest. It was a question of class, and I think that the North American public should understand that it was largely an economic question.

The persecution gradually became more systematic and real. The right-wing women, the fascist women, gathered in a final meeting in front of the Catholic University, and the slogan of the day was "Out with the foreigners, death to the foreigners." *La Segunda,* for example, published articles saying that "Jews were the disgrace of the world" and printed articles against prominent Chilean Jews such as Jaime Faivovich, the under-secretary of transport, Volodia Teitelboim, a leader of the CP, and David Silberman, manager of the Chuquicamata mine. The published articles against Jews and foreigners, classifying them in the same way.

On September 11, I woke up at 7:30. I left the house in an effort to go where I was supposed to be— with the people who gave us affection and welcomed us. My factory was located fairly close to Technical University, and by 8:15 the Tacna Regiment had already cordoned off the area. I was almost taken prisoner but managed to escape along with some others and arrive at my job. Then the bombardment of Technical University began and many *compañeros* were taken prisoner. The cannons and .30-caliber machine guns later took up positions in front of our factory and opened fire. The workers resisted, not for the mere sake of resisting, but in defense of the rights they had won: to elect their own president and representatives, to have social improvements, for the right of their women to the same conditions enjoyed by bourgeois women, for their children to go to school, to defend the interests of democracy, of the constitution, of a more just society. The workers struggled and resisted as best they could in that factory. Many *compañeros* were taken prisoner and shot on the spot, without trial, without anything. Those who managed to escape went to other places.

Several *compañeros* and I fled to the Cordón San Joaquín

[San Joaquín industrial belt]. We arrived at around one in the afternoon — just as the military began bombarding and machine-gunning it. Children were crying in the streets. Old people prayed to God because they did not understand what was happening. The workers fought. The women and children, brothers, and people of their class fought. It was a totally spontaneous resistance, but it was heroic. The bombardment was indiscriminate. People were dying — kids, pregnant women — it was total chaos, with screaming that no one understood. It is very difficult to describe the total chaos and confusion. The military seized the Luchetti factory. They shot the president and vice president of the union (one was in the Communist Party, the other in the Socialist Party), and took various *compañeros* prisoners. But people managed to flee from there and organize another type of resistance in another place. They were shot down like animals, but they died defending their interests, defending their right to build a new country.

While the working class neighborhoods were being bombarded there were celebrations in Providencia. The bourgeois houses put flags on the doors, rejoicing at the coup, rejoicing at the death of the people in the *poblaciones*. They even lynched a Black Panamanian who was walking down the street, who didn't even know about the coup. They took him and lynched him.

People fought as best they could, and when they could resist no more they fled to save their own lives. There was nothing else left to do. We managed to escape this harsh fire after a few hours, but it seemed like a century of bombing, like a century of people dying there. We managed to enter a house and stayed there. My own house was later invaded by the fascists, not by the armed forces themselves, but rather civilians of the Patria y Libertad party. It must be stressed, however, that although the Christian Democratic Party supported the coup, there were working people among the Christian Democrats who were resisting along with us in the factories.

Denunciations were a common thing. The military called for the betrayal of all foreigners living in Chile. Military helicopters dropped leaflets all over Santiago that said, "The foreigners came to Chile to kill, to assassinate — find and denounce them."

I went to seek asylum in an embassy. There was nothing else left to do. The coup had succeeded, everything was chaotic.

Practically all our houses were searched, ransacked. We were all betrayed. With the help of some other *compañeros,* we managed to get to the Mexican Embassy where we found the safety deserved by any citizen, regardless of his race or ideology — as a human being.

But there were thousands of us in Chile, and many did not find safety in embassies. Many foreigners who lived in the San Borja Towers were arrested and taken to the National Stadium. Two hundred and fifty Bolivians were rounded up and sent back to their country. I can imagine what their fate was when they were handed over to the dictators who had persecuted them in Bolivia.

I wonder if the North Americans — sitting in their homes, watching TV and peacefully eating what the workers in Latin America produce — really know how these workers are being persecuted, are being actually shot down in the streets? Does the average citizen of the silent majority really know what is going on in Latin America — the dictatorships, the military governments, the last coup?

The American people must be made to know what is going on in Chile. And it is important that in the U.S. there is an effective means of combating what happened in Chile in terms of international pressure, because fascism doesn't care much about international pressure from democratic forces. In Chile there will be seen the consequences of what is happening throughout the world but very little compared to what would happen if the U.S. pressured Chile. And so I think that the workers, students, progressives, and democrats from the States have the most effective means to stop the summary executions that are going on in Chile. They must wage such a campaign that they force the U.S. government to come out against the repression. In other words, that Chile's master try to put the brakes on what's happening there. It's more than political; it's psychological. One respects the voice of one's master.

JOSE

[José, forty-two, has been a member of the Chilean Communist Party for more than fifteen years. He worked in the Indugas factory in the Cordón O'Higgins in Santiago.]

One of the important problems under the Allende government was the shortage of bottled gas, but this can only be described as a right-wing maneuver. Our factory made gas cylinders. There was no lack of materials to make them, and at no time did the cylinder line stop producing. The cylinders then left the factory, but I don't know where they went. Later on the filling of the cylinders with gas began to slacken. It's known that they blamed it on the production of cylinders, but I know that's incorrect because I was a worker there and could see that the production was going well.

On September 11 we were working as usual in the factory when we heard some huge explosions. At first we thought that some gas cylinders had exploded, so we stayed inside. But soon the explosions started again. We went outside to look, just as the planes began to pass overhead. The *compañeros* with radios heard the news, and we realized that La Moneda was being attacked. Then the factory intervenor called us all to a meeting and explained that there appeared to be a coup occurring but that he couldn't be sure since the radio had stropped transmitting, except to play music. Later, about 11:00 a.m. we met again and the intervenor stated definitely that it was a military coup. No one knew what to do, we all felt crushed. The intervenor said that it just couldn't happen in Chile, and asked what we could do. He called together all of

89

the leaders of the employees and operators, and of the union. We decided that we should go to our homes. We could do nothing in the factory since we didn't really know where we stood, nor were we in contact with any other people. The intervenor adjourned the meeting and told us to go. We were all grief-stricken, especially those of us who had always stood on the side of Allende. We left bitter at our impotence, our inability to act to help our government. We were totally defenseless. Many have said that we had a fantastic arsenal in the factory, but we didn't even have a single revolver. The only revolver belonged to one of the factory watchmen.

I went straight home that day. From the terrace on the third floor of my house I could see La Moneda and the adjacent buildings in flames. The shelling was over and the radio was calling for firemen to come and put out the flames. Bullets were flying all around. It was a state of siege until the government actually fell at about 6:00 p.m. Afterwards one couldn't go out into the streets, as there was shooting in all directions. I lived near the Burguer factory, which had only recently been nationalized. I was so close I could feel it when they machine-gunned the people there, because they had stayed in the factory. Many women worked there. From some *compañeras* who were working there I heard that many were killed. Some were leaders. The intervenor was taken prisoner, and the union president was shot in front of all the women. They gave the women workers five seconds to leave. Those who could, saved themselves from the hail of bullets. Those who could get into the houses near the factory got out of it alive, the rest fell to the ground. Nothing mattered, they didn't care that they were women, young women with children. They respected nothing.

The following day the bakeries by my house began to sell, since the people were desparate for food. I could see how the *carabineros* shot people on the lines.

To get back to what happened at the factory where I worked. Many *compañeros* listened to the call made by the fascist Junta for workers to report to their factories. They said that there would be no repressive actions taken, that they shouldn't be afraid, nothing would be done to them. All of the workers went to the factory. In the factory we found that the old boss and the production manager, who's a fascist German, had returned. They had us wait there a whole day without calling us in. We were told to come back the following day. The next day they began to pay some attention to us. There were two lists. They made us enter the factory in groups of ten. There was a troop of *carabineros* armed with machine guns inside the factory. The boss and the production manager gave a lecture to all the workers — employees and operators. They went in submissive, with their heads lowered, like slaves. This went on until about ninety of us remained outside. Later, twenty of these *compañeros* were taken inside for several hours, after which they were arrested. I was in a group of *compañeros* with whom I usually worked, when I realized that the others, the ones who had been arrested, had been taken to the National Stadium. From the section I worked in they took five *compañeros;* I was the only one spared. Seeing this I decided to give up everything for lost and get out.

Before the coup the factory had been searched. They treated us like criminals. We had to stand out on the factory patio, in the sun, for five hours. Once in a while they would call someone and strip him in front of everyone, to see if he was armed. But there were really no weapons in our factory. There had been rumors circulated that we were manufacturing arms. I worked some night shifts so I'm sure that we made no arms. It was because of the arms question that they came in to beat us, all of us. There were no class distinctions there, one could be a Christian Democrat or what have you. They even called women out and stripped them.

They are already persecuting even the rank-and-file *compañeros* who supported the Unidad Popular. *Compañeros* of the Christian Democratic Party and other tendencies are also suffering this harassment. The repression in Chile is not just against one political party, it is against the entire working class.

As far as I know, three of us from my factory took asylum — myself and two others. I was the first and I helped the others to find asylum. We went to the factory and were among the last to enter so we were able to find out that they were taking some of the *compañeros* to the stadium. One of the *compañeros* told us that the Mexican Embassy was receiving exiles. So we went there.

I am married and have a sixteen-year-old daughter. Now that I am here, I think mostly about my family. I feel great helplessness in not knowing what is happening to them, not knowing how they are.

Unfortunately our government did not take a hard hand against the fascists. It could have used a hard hand against the military after the *tancazo*. They could have done it because the great majority of workers, no matter what party they were in, were against this military action. So, with this base, with such a strong backing from the working class, from the people, the government really had all the force and power it needed to stop what the fascists were trying to do. But instead the regime continued as it had begun — doing everything in a peaceful way. But those of us who were rank and filers saw how the struggle really was, and we knew what form the struggle had to take.

Many of us workers who were conscious of the process believed that the government did not want a class fight because it wanted to avoid a massacre, because the workers, the people, would be the ones hurt by it. For that reason it did not want to strike in the way the workers wanted — with a hard hand.

And so this is how it was lost. Now we have to flee to other countries, without knowing how our families are, humiliated more than ever. We have lost everything we won in more than one hundred years of struggle. All this was taken from us by this military fascist coup. For us, for those on the left, and I believe for the majority of the people, these fascists are butchers, assassins.

But we have to remember that everything is not lost; that there are people who continue struggling. There are *compañeros* in the industries who are going to continue to fight. This I know for sure. Because the consciousness of the worker has not been destroyed. We are accustomed to suffering.

HUGO BLANCO

[Hugo Blanco, a principal organizer of the peasant movement in Peru, was arrested in 1963 and sentenced to twenty-five years in prison for his organizing activities in that country. Released from prison in 1970 under the pressure of an international campaign, Blanco was expelled from Peru in 1971. After spending some time in Mexico, he went to Argentina in June 1972 and was arrested by the military authorities in July. He remained in prison until October 1972, at which time he was able to go to Chile. Blanco is a leading Latin American supporter of the Trotskyist Fourth International.]

In 1971 I was deported from Peru. Nine months later I traveled to Argentina on a tourist visa and after one month there I was seized and put in jail by the Argentine police. No charges were ever brought against me, nor was I told the reasons for my arrest. I was questioned about my political past in Peru, but not about anything connected with Argentine politics. What they wanted was for me to leave the country. But since I had entered on a three-month permit, I defended my legal right to remain. This proved fruitless; the military government paid no attention to the laws on the books while it was in power. Once again I had to start looking for a country that would accept me. The only thing we were able to come up with at that time was asylum; no, not asylum, but that Chile would accept me on a fifteen-day transit visa,

en route to a third country. As soon as I got to Chile I made
it clear to the authorities that I had no intention of choosing
yet another country, and that I wanted permission to remain
as a political exile. They approved my request, and gave me
a resident visa for one year, expiring in January 1974. In
other words, I was in Chile legally. I even had a Chilean
identity card.

Perhaps I should double back and talk about prison conditions in Argentina because the conditions of political prisoners in that country are not well known. I had been in jail
in Peru for long periods, but the treatment of prisoners in
Argentina is much worse, not so much from the physical point
of view but in terms of morale. In their attempt to crush the
prison population the forces of repression maintain something
even worse than barracks discipline. There's a lot to be
said here.

I was kept in isolation for several days, and then spent
several days with other prisoners. In both cases the extent
of the repression was acutely visible. You have to remember
that they had nothing special against me; all they wanted was
to get me out of the country. I hadn't participated at all in
Argentine politics, and their treatment of me was in no way
different from their usual way of dealing with political prisoners. Certainly there must have been some who were treated
more violently, but I was not among them.

For example, there were the infamous *pesquisas* [searches].
When I was in Argentina the guards would enter the cells
every once in a while to look for weapons, metal objects or
whatever might be hidden. They would go through the contents of all the cells. Inevitably, each cell would be left in complete disorder. For example, we were housed in groups of
ten prisoners. Some of our comrades would be cooking, some
in the bathroom, some washing clothes, when a bunch of
guards would come toward the door of the building and order
us to run toward the back with our hands behind our backs.
Whatever we were doing we had to stop on the spot and run,
hands behind our backs, and no talking. Then they would
call us one by one and make us take off all our clothes and
squat on the floor while they examined our rectums and looked
under our testicles. Then they would order us to carry our
clothing and march naked to another building, there other
guards made us dress quickly and line up with our faces to

the wall and our hands behind our backs and no talking. Meanwhile they were going through our cells. After two hours we would return to our cells, where we would find everything in chaos. Those who had been cooking found the food strewn all over the floor mixed with garbage; clothing and personal effects were all mixed in with the garbage and food.

Prisoners were allowed to do some manual work. In Peru this was never allowed, but in Argentina prisoners were permitted to work in wood and leather. When we would return to our cells, all of this craftwork would be missing, including the tools, which had been obtained only after enormous delays, red tape, etc. Often watches, books, and other things were thrown on the floor. They did this to infuriate the prisoners and keep them in a state of constant tension.

These *pesquisas* were routine, so that the prisoners were unable to lead normal, stable, peaceful lives in prison, despite the rules which were supposed to restrict the guards. There also were times when the guards refused to admit any visitors or to let us speak with our lawyers. In my own case for example, I received a telegram of solidarity. It was delivered to me, but later, when I tried to give it to my lawyer, they took it away from me.

The repression against the Argentine prisoners was much worse. There was one prisoner who had been sent a radio. They called him over the loud speaker and he had no idea whether it was because he had a visitor, or to see his lawyer, or a change of cell, or what. They do this to keep people in suspense. Then they took him off with other prisoners who had come from other buildings, forbidden to look anywhere but straight ahead. They had to walk through long corridors with the terror of now knowing where they were going or why. Then they separated him out and told him that they were going to give him something his family had brought. When they reached the room where gifts from relatives were distributed they showed him the radio, and they told him, "This radio is from your family." As he moved forward to accept it, they dropped it on the floor, smashing it to pieces. The guard said it was a shame and that he should go back to his cell.

Things like this show the cruelty of the guards toward political prisoners. In other sections the guards steal, but that's it, or at most they say that things got lost. But not here. This is an example of how they act toward political prisoners. In the "punishment" cells they keep them naked; and the floors are wet. They get terrible food, and they're forbidden to read or smoke. You could be sent to the punishment room for any little thing — because a guard decided you hadn't run fast enough or for any other reason. The atmosphere was much worse after the Trelew massacre. [On August 15, 1972, twenty-five Argentine political prisoners staged a jail break. Nineteen were quickly recaptured and taken to Trelew air base. On August 22, Argentine marines opened fire on them, killing sixteen and wounding three.]

Another terrible thing was the kind of dungeon they put you in before you actually entered the jail, or where you went on any errands. They were cells where you had no idea how long you would be there. They weren't considered punishment cells, but rather a type of waiting room where people stayed while some sort of transaction was being effected. If a person stretched out on a blanket, he could barely fit inside these cells, and smoking and reading were prohibited. Before you were put in they took away your watch, your shoes, your belt, your shoelaces. It was real torture, because days and nights went by and there was no way of telling what time of day it was since there was no light. Once a day you were allowed a visit to the bathroom. The only variation was in the small and lousy meals they gave. The prisoners spent days on end in terrible anxiety. For me it was nothing serious, just annoying. But you have to remember that they used these cells for the people who were awaiting torture. One of the times they sent me there, since I wasn't that important, they threw me in a common cell with a lot of other prisoners. From there we could see the prisoners from the individual cells being marched to the interrogation rooms, and we saw them return covered with blood, with blood spurting from their clothes, some limping or with their arms paralyzed. There was no medical care given; they didn't even give them clean clothes after wounding them. And they stayed like that. We also could hear the screams of those who were being tortured. As I said, my own situation was one of the best. I knew all they wanted was to get me off their hands. so I never underwent intensive grilling. They didn't ask me anything about what I had been doing in Argentina. They did ask me about my political past, but only in a very general way. That was all. But the fate of the Argentine prisoners was atrocious, both in the individual cells from where they were taken to be tortured and in the main prison where they also tortured people.

I heard macabre stories from my *compañeros* about the tortures that went on in the dungeons of the fort. They were basically beatings, although they also used dunking. Besides dunking them in huge deposits of excrement, as they do to the Chilean peasants and to prisoners in other places, they also used electricity. They would stick things up the ass, and up women's vaginas. I spoke with an Argentine woman in Chile, whose baby had died in jail a month after birth because of the terrible conditions she had been kept in up to a month before it was born. When they finally took her to the maternity ward they handcuffed her to the cot, and certainly all these things must have affected the child who had no way of resisting and died after a month. This *compañera* was very stunned by the death, she couldn't get over the death of her baby.

Well, that is basically what I saw in the Argentine jail, and I want to say once more that there was nothing special done to me personally; that those who really suffered were the Argentine *compañeros* who were the ones the whole thing had been set up to get. All I did was share general prison conditions with them. In October 1972 I was expelled from Argentina and sent to Chile, and I received asylum there.

It would take a long time to recount everything I saw in the eleven months I was in Chile. I'm just going to talk about the last things that happened. The night before the coup I had slept in a settlement on the outskirts of town, and in the morning I took the bus along with the workers who were on their way to work. There was nothing out of the ordinary among either the workers or any of the other passengers. In other words, nobody was aware of anything unusual having to do with a coup. When the bus reached Plaza Bulnes I got off, and as I passed the Ministry of Defense I was surprised to see soldiers coming out. They were telling the people to make way so they could surround the Ministry. At first I thought maybe it was because of a housewives' demonstration and that it was a way of preventing any acts of provocation by the fascists, who had recently been out in force pro-

testing against General Prats and the officers who were
ministers in Allende's government.

So, with this interpretation in mind I went on along the
streets of Santiago to the house of a friend I was supposed
to see. I saw a lot of people on foot, which surprised me
although I knew there was a transit strike and people had
been walking to work. But there were more people walking
than normal, since the strike was incomplete. There was an
odd, congested atmosphere. I heard some elegant young people listening to their radios and I saw happiness on their
faces. They were saying how optimistic they felt. Later, on
my way toward the Mapocho River, I happened to overhear
the radio of another pedestrian, where they were talking about
the incapacity of the military to govern. This surprised me.
Since neither the left nor the right would say anything like
that; it seemed strange to me. Then in passing I heard a sen-
tence about the Military Junta. Right then, I understood what
was going on. The coup we had all been expecting had occurred. Everybody knew a coup was coming, we didn't know
when it would be or of what magnitude. Without a doubt,
the coup had taken place. I arrived at my friend's house where
we were still able to catch something on his radio. It was
a pro-government station which was saying that the workers had to remain on alert, but it wasn't giving complete instructions. We also heard some Junta-controlled stations, on
which they announced that a curfew would go into effect at
three. Before this I had gone to the post office to mail a letter,
but it was closed. And in midtown I had seen a *carabinero*
tell a woman to close her newspaper stand. These things had
happened before I knew about the coup. Since there was a
three o'clock deadline for people to be in their homes, I had
to start home immediately because I lived thirty-five blocks
from where I was and most buses weren't running. So I started walking.

The atmosphere on the street was one of total chaos, like
I had seen in the streets of Cuzco, Peru, after the 1950 earth-
quake. That is the only possible comparison for what I saw
in Chile, such shock on people's faces on account of what
was happening. Even though the danger of a coup had been
in the air for quite a while, people were still confused. I didn't
see any happy faces in the section of town I was in. I'm sure
there were some people who were glad, but in an atmosphere

of such uncertainty they were probably afraid to show their happiness in the crowded streets where most people had sadness and shock on their faces. I passed a hospital door where some fellows were handing out flyers. It surprised me that the left should have been able to mobilize so fast and that they were already turning out literature about the issue, but when I read the flyer I saw that they were from a previous time. They were about the actions of the fascists, urging the armed forces to crush fascist acts — flyers of the Communist Party. Most likely the rank-and-file Communist Party members who worked in that hospital, feeling a sense of desperation and impotence, had begun distributing these outdated flyers which they had on hand. In any case, it was obvious that the people who got them were reading them avidly.

Since I figured we were going to be stuck in our houses, I had bought a dozen eggs before arriving at my house. I got there just at the hour of the curfew. Later, several radio stations announced that the curfew would begin at six. The first announcement had been that it would start at three. My son and the mother of my daughter were listening to the radio. I lived with my two children who were in school in Chile. My fourteen-year-old daughter especially loved Chile because it is the Latin American country with perhaps the most openness and least hypocrisy, and the people are tremendously warm. My daughter would tell me that she felt more Chilean than Peruvian. And she had only been in Chile a few months. She liked what they taught in school, and she was doing well despite the fact that I didn't have much time to help her. She was very interested in the social sciences, and that is what is so different from what they teach in the rest of Latin America. It was a much more human way of teaching, one that had to do with actual human problems.

Two days before the coup the mother of my daughter had arrived, planning to stay for a week or two, but it turned out she was only able to be there freely for two days, Sunday and Monday. The coup was on Tuesday, so from three o'clock on we were inside our house burning all papers that might be considered suspicious. From the announcements we had heard on the radio we could already sense the ferocity of this coup, in other words, it wasn't an ordinary run-of-the-mill coup like others that have taken place in Latin America. I was in Argentina during the coup against Perón, and it didn't come near the Chilean coup in ferocity. My daughter, with great sorrow, had to take down her posters and burn her papers and magazines. I realized that possession of any of the flyers that had been handed out so freely in the streets up to the day before, or any paper bought at a newsstand, or the posters that everybody had, could do us in.

We were listening to the radio. We were very tense. Next door there was a house—well, bourgeois—where they were listening to and commenting with great joy about the announcements. Even when it was announced that there were snipers who were resisting and that if they didn't turn themselves in by five o'clock they wouldn't have another chance but would be shot on the spot, even then we could hear the shouts of joy and approval of the bourgeois who lived next to us. They were the type who have three or four servants and a very clear class consciousness. From the patio of the house I lived in we saw the planes that were bombing La Moneda. We saw the bombing, and I suppose we also saw in the other direction where the planes were heading toward Tomás Moro, Allende's residence. Later we heard the announcement of Allende's death. My daughter couldn't hold back any more and she began to cry inconsolably when she heard.

Later on the junta urged those who were patriotic to put flags on their houses. From the window we saw many houses with flags up, whether out of fear of whatever. But after the news of Allende's death and other news—although it was news given by the junta—the next day we saw the flags being taken down from some houses. I heard that in one neighborhood some leftist boys, full of fury, burned the flags of those who wanted to show their joy at the coup, and that they were seen by a military patrol and immediately executed.

Wednesday too was a day of constant tension. We couldn't go outside because the curfew wasn't lifted until twelve o'clock on Thursday. So from three o'clock Tuesday until twelve on Thursday we were shut in the house, and this was the same for everyone. And with enormous anxiety, because to go outside meant liquidation, being shot; and besides, there was the fear that at any moment the police or the army would arrive and raze the house or kill somebody or take us prisoner. In other words we couldn't move at all.

On Wednesday I heard blows on the door. I thought it was the police, so I went out to take care of the problem, but it was a woman, the president of our local Junta de Abastecimiento y Precios [Supply and Price Committee] The JAPs were neighborhood groups organized to combat black marketing of basic necessities, and to control prices, directly distribute scarce commodities, etc. This woman felt she should go on with her duty of distributing ration cards, and had come to give us our coupon for a kilo of sugar. She was doing it on the run, knowing that she could be shot at any moment, but she felt she had an obligation toward the neighbors. Of course the next day or the day after they dissolved the JAPs and price control committees. Well, since there was this tremendous tension, I began to make a domino game out of cardboard to play with my kids to distract them a little. The nervous tension was hurting everyone. It was impossible to concentrate even on reading. There was nothing to do, shut in the way we were, except wait for the arrival of the police or the army.

On Thursday morning I took out my typewriter and just before the curfew was lifted I wrote out something for the *compañeros* — some of the last things I wanted to tell them, for I wasn't sure whether I was going to die in the coming days or not. Since nobody in Chile was safe, I left it to my daughter to find some way of making sure it got to Peru or elsewhere. After doing that, I said goodbye to all of them, spelling out just how our contact would be maintained, and that they had to return to Peru. Of course they understood that they could not show up at the Peruvian Embassy before my whereabouts were publicly known, since it was quite possible they would be tortured to make them tell where I was hiding. But I told them that as soon as it was made public where I was, they should go to the Peruvian Embassy so they would be able to go back to Peru.

Then I left and went to the house of a friend who had had nothing to do with politics, and I hid there for two or three days, I'm not sure exactly. From her house, just as from mine and from the embassy where I was later, we could hear gunfire during the night, and we even heard someone walking on the roof. It seems that in the area of my friend's house there was still some sniping, even during the day. After the curfew was lifted and people lined up for bread the next morning, there were corpses on the street, and the people in line were talking about what was happening. It was really strange, since most of the people were silent; but whenever someone would start to talk about the atrocities, other people would join in. The soldiers who were standing guard must certainly have responded with violence whenever any protest started up.

My daughter later told me—when I saw her again—that when they were baking the bread in the area we lived in a little boy stuck his tongue out at a *carabinero* who was watching the line and that the *carabinero* replied by striking him in the face with his gun butt.

Later, in the Mexican Embassy, where a number of us found refuge, I saw that many people who tried to get into the embassy were turned away and taken prisoner. Among them some of my *compañeros* recognized Allende's chauffer. When I was in the embassy I learned that my name and where I was had appeared in the Swedish press, and I managed to get through to my children and to the mother of my daughter so that they could all go to the Peruvian Embassy. They got out along with other Peruvians and are now in Peru.

EDUARDO CREUS

[Eduardo Creus is an Argentine Trotskyist journalist. In 1963 he was participating in the Peruvian revolutionary movement when he was arrested and sentenced to seventeen years in prison. Creus was released from jail in 1971, after a major international support campaign, and returned to Argentina. He had gone to Chile in May 1973 to analyze the Chilean process and write articles for *Avanzada Socialista*, the weekly newspaper of the Argentine Socialist Workers Party.]

Because of the curfew on September 11 I had to remain in the zone where I lived, conversing with the people, seeing the populace's state of mind — anguish and doubt about what was happening, waiting for those who were to instruct them. The curfew was originally called for 3:00 p.m., but began at 5:00 p.m. because the junta extended it two hours to give more time to people who were far from their homes and had to travel. After 5:00, leaving the house was impossible. You couldn't even peek out the door because police patrols started in my neighborhood, forcing everyone to remain inside. At nightfall there was surveillance by copters and land vehicles, and you heard shooting, ceaselessly, small caliber arms against big ones, especially machine guns. You heard people running and machine-gun noises. From that moment the curfew, which lasted around forty-eight hours, prevented people from getting information from outside; they had only the radio, which was now entirely in the hands of the Military Junta. The stations formed one solid network and continually broadcast the Junta's reports and decrees. At home I heard the third or fourth decree, ordering that anyone knowing the whereabouts of foreign residents must denounce them. Obviously this put me in a precarious position, since I was well known in the neighborhood as a foreigner. But the residents there were as worried about me as I was, telling me to be careful, not to go out or show myself so nothing would happen to me. I pointed this out because all these working people came over now and then to inform me of troop movements. I was once even warned that the neighborhood was being "flattened." So I had to leave and take refuge in a friend's house. This was when the permanent curfew has already been lifted and was enforced only intermittently through the day. I stayed there about four days and heard from witnesses about assorted cases of military repression. These cases involved residents getting in line earlier than allowed at bakeries or the centers where bread was usually distributed. Since the streets were patrolled, when the troops approached, the people in line were terrified — because the soldiers began to shoot. So they ran and didn't heed the soldiers' orders to halt. Two people on bread lines were killed this way.

One noteworthy case which revealed the advanced sectors' determination to confront the coup, even if it could only be done piecemeal, involved three workers from an area next to mine. They went out during the first two nights of total curfew and disarmed sentries in the streets and seized some machine guns. They kept this up until meeting up with a squad of soldiers, at which point they were shot down. The arms they had already taken from the soldiers were used two nights later by a group of workers in that neighborhood to attack the planes doing surveillance by night.

They brought one down. I know personally that it was shot down because I was still awake at 2:00 a.m. when this plane, and others, made low-flying raids to frighten the population or bomb some sector or other. We would hear them every night. The planes passed low overhead and then I heard a burst of machine-gun fire and a plane crash. It was also totally confirmed by the subsequent leveling of the zone where it fell. After this the low-flying night flights stopped and the helicopters began flying much higher to avoid machine-gun fire.

The next morning, all the areas where these sharpshooters were imagined to be holed up were razed; not one house was spared; and the troops sacked them all, taking everything of value and all the money they found. (Besides the money stored in a professor's place, they carried off all of his equipment).

On the fourth or fifth day in the besieged neighborhood where I lived, a few local activists mobilized to warn known members of the right wing not to turn in any leader or activist. This worked and, in general, there were no betrayals in this area because these militants organized to prevent it. But there was one case where a member of the Movimiento de Izquierda Revolucionaria [MIR] personally warned a neighborhood merchant to be very careful about handing in any lists, because the merchant knew all the leftist leaders, and his reactionary position was known. This merchant didn't react well, and turned in the man who had threatened him. The activist was arrested immediately and taken to an unknown location.

There were constant arrests in the area, on any pretext. For instance, two workers (one a Communist Party member and neighborhood leader, the other an independent) were arrested and taken to an improvised barracks in a school, because some soldiers had been chasing some girls, and the girls got scared and ran into various houses, and those who hid in these two workers' places were arrested with them. Later, they released the girls but kept the men in the barracks. Afterwards the independent was freed and the Communist was transferred to the National Stadium, according to neighborhood reports.

As I mentioned before, I had been warned that the neighborhood was going to be razed, so I moved to a house in a different area. The Junta kept insisting and demanding that the population turn in the foreigners. Realizing that my situation was more and more delicate, I was forced to seek asylum in the Mexican Embassy.

The situation was the same in the second house I hid in as in the neighborhood where I had lived before. Not one night went by without skirmishes and constant violent shooting with all sorts of weapons.

After staying in this house and seeking a permanent refuge, I went out to look over the city on a bus (mass transit had begun to function in a very limited way). I could confirm the destruction the armed forces had inflicted on the businesses and factories. For instance in the Municipalidad de la Cisterna the surrounding buildings were completely machine-gunned and some obviously had been hit by tank cannons. Transit was closed off in different zones occupied by the troops, where apparently there was resistance, as in the case of the Sumar factory or the nearby Gran Avenida. The Municipalidad de la Cisterna clearly put up strong resistance, to judge by the machine-gun damage and the cannon attacks on the municipal offices.

Many residents of my neighborhood still didn't know where their relatives were on the fourth day of the coup. This naturally caused enormous concern, for many might be dead, or prisoners in the concentration camps, or in the stadium where the greatest concentration of prisoners are arrested people were held.

Before seeking asylum in the Mexican Embassy I was able to establish contact with a worker from Cordón Cerrillos, a member of the leadership of a factory, who told me that though he had tried to communicate with the leadership he couldn't because they had to all intents and purposes disappeared. He said he was well-known and afraid for his life; so he asked me what to do. He was hoping to take refuge in some embassy, in view of the futility of all resistance, at least at the level of the workers' boards and occupied industries. Later I ran into that same man as a refugee in Mexico City. He said he had left because his life was really in danger, that numerous workers were being arrested. This is undoubtedly true. I discovered through talks with many exiled workers that they had gone back later to their factories to collect their biweekly pay, but they were prevented from entering and could not even get their back salaries. The majority of these workers (especially the best known and the activists) therefore decided not to return to their plants, because they realized that the next step would be their arrest. As we know from the mouth of the Junta itself, around 15 percent of the workers in all these formerly occupied factories have been suspended — those marked as activists or leaders of the factories and the workers' management boards.

Obviously there was resistance. It took place on at least two levels. On the one hand it was carried out by the groups closest to the government such as the GAP [Grupo de Amigos Personales — Group of Personal Friends] which was an organization of ex-guerrillas who had pledged to defend Allende and by the fighting groups of the Socialist Party and other sections of the UP. On the other hand there was spontaneous resistance carried out by neighborhood workers, usually belonging to the MIR. But I must point out that at no point was resistance organized by the MIR leadership. The resistance was localized, spontaneous, and mostly independent.

HERNANDO LABBE

[Hernando Labbé, twenty-five, is a Chilean, who was in charge of a production line at the Indugas factory. Active in his trade union, he was not affiliated with any political party.]

On the day of the coup, I was at work. At a meeting of the intervenor and the workers we decided not to occupy the factory, not to leave the workers at their posts. I think it would have been an error to keep people there. If we had stayed there would have been an incredibly savage massacre. We had absolutely nothing to defend ourselves with, not even a matchstick. What could we do? It would have been like a fight between a lion and a puppy.

On Friday, September 14, there was a call to return to the factory — they called only the line heads. I didn't show up because I was wounded. I had been shot twice in the shoulder. There would have been no chance for me to work anyhow. I had been a union leader the year before and there was a case against me for usurpation of property; I was accused of having illegally used the factory, which meant there was a criminal charge and arrest order against me. Besides, when they called us to the factory to regularize our situation there was no opportunity for us to work. When people got there, they were taken prisoner and hauled away.

As I mentioned, I had been shot. It happened on Sunday, September 16, about 2:00 p.m. We were living at my parent's house for the safety of my family. We had gone to my house to pick up toys and things to entertain the children and were on our way back. About 2:00 we passed a military patrol in front of a factory that had been attacked the day before, even though there had been a search previously — the workers had invited the authorities to go through and verify that there were no arms there. Anyhow, I drove by there, in front of the patrol. They didn't tell me to stop. I was going at a reasonable speed. But once we were on the bridge, they shot at me, to kill. That's the truth. I have two bullets in my shoulder, near my head, as proof. If they had hit me in the head the car would have gone off the bridge with my wife in it; they would have destroyed the family all at once.

And those pigs — when I asked them why they shot at me, they wouldn't answer; they just looked over my shoulder and made a taxi stop for me. Later my father and father-in-law went to pick up the car and they apologized — it had been a mistake. They were nervous from having gone so long without sleep. Those imbeciles. It didn't matter to them that they could have destroyed a family. It could have been a tragedy for my family, for my wife's family. They could have stopped me with a shot in the air or in one of the tires. But no, another person's life didn't matter to them — only killing mattered.

Something similar happened in my father's workshop. He has an auto repair shop. The other day a customer stopped to pick up his car. As he was starting up the car, the military told him to stop, but since he was deaf he couldn't hear them. So without another word they riddled him with bullets and that was that — it was over.

Anyhow, I was lucky, the two bullets passed through the car and that slowed them down. If they had struck me full force, they would have ripped my arm off. As it is I have trouble moving it.

When I got to the first aid station I explained what had happened and they took care of me. There weren't very many people there that Sunday, but the *compañero* who took me to the first aid station — he works on an ambulance and is used to such things — told me that he had gotten really sick seeing so much horror and savagery against the people. He was completely traumatized. He couldn't take it anymore — even a person who was hardened to it couldn't stand to see so many deaths. It was unthinkable — children, women, students; they respected absolutely nothing. They are real savages. I don't think that anywhere else in the world they have moved with such savagery against a totally defenseless working class. It would have been different, I think, if we had been prepared.

I don't think it's the common soldiers who hate us — they're from the same class. It's those in command of the armed forces who feel the bitterness, the hatred. It was the first time the workers had a chance to organize, to direct an enterprise. All of a sudden it was the commanders who had to obey orders, not the common soldiers. They saw the changes taking place in Chile — the poorest sectors of the population assuming more and more responsibility, getting into the structure of capitalist production, etc. That was the source of their hatred.

PATRICIO

[Patricio was a paramedic at the Barros Luco Hospital in Santiago. He was well known for his volunteer medical work in the *campamentos,* the shanty-towns built by squatters, and also from appearances on television where he had been interviewed on a number of occasions about bodies of victims assassinated by Patria y Libertad terrorists.]

At the hospital, when we got news of the coup, we immediately met and took our emergency posts and began to treat the wounded who were brought in by the hundreds from the Cordón Santa Rosa. By night time, there were thousands of wounded and dead. The first day we counted 1800 dead in the Institute of Medical Pathology. In a six-hour shift, I myself counted 538 dead, and other *compañeros* counted the rest. Later, the military took over the hospital, threw away the food, raped the women who were working, robbed the blood bank, and stole jewelry, money, and everything else they could lay their hands on. They only allowed the military to be treated, not civilians.

There was a case of an eleven-year-old girl who arrived with her parents. She had a .50-caliber projectile in her leg. She was unconscious and we had to amputate the leg immediately. We asked her mother and father to donate blood for the operation. They did, but we couldn't perform the operation because the *carabineros* took the blood. We collected more blood for the operation from the hospital staff, but it was already too late. The child died.

The military took over the hospital in their own special way, as they had in all the factories. They came saying that there were snipers there, which was totally false. The snipers were the *carabineros* who had murdered forty workers at the Concha y Toro winery. They murdered all of them. They left the doors and windows open and the corpses were on top of the pipes. Some were hanging; some had been beaten; some were without heads; others were without arms. I went there with the hospital's priest and saw what had happened.

We decided not to leave the hospital but to stay and work. When we opposed the military's policy of taking bood from civilians, they pointed machine guns at us and placed tanks at the door of the public clinic and at the main door. They told us that if we didn't keep taking blood from civilians, they'd kill everyone. We told them we'd prefer that they kill us but that they should allow the many young people who were dying to live. You couldn't call these young people guerrillas because they had no weapons.

We asked the military to let us treat civilians. Their answer was to place more tanks at the door and to make us work with machine guns aimed at our backs and heads. There were three soldiers or *carabineros* guarding each of us. Wherever we went they guarded us.

After two days the right-wing doctors, who had been on strike, arrived to take possession of their posts. They came with people from the Patria y Libertad movement. Later the junta declared that the "heroes" of Patria y Libertad had dissolved their movement because it is now the junta.

JURANDIR ANTONIO XAVIER

[Jurandir Antonio Xavier, twenty-seven, is a Brazilian from São Paulo.]

I began my university studies in 1965. My family was poor, of middle-class rural origins. After a series of problems we had in trying to keep up the production on our small farm, we had to uproot ourselves and move to São Paulo to try to make a go of it there. I succeeded in entering the university, which is quite a difficult thing to do in Brazil.

After President João Goulart was overthrown and a military dictatorship established in 1964, the dictatorship began a campaign of fierce repression against the poorest sectors of the population and against the student vanguard, which had carried out important mobilizations in Brazil in 1964. In the economic field the dictatorship opened the country up to foreign capital, mainly North American. This drove Brazilian-owned industry into a disastrous condition.

In the university arena, a pact was signed by the Minister of Education and Culture and the U.S. Agency for International Development (AID), placing the university under U.S. control. Beginning in 1965 and 1966 we began a campaign in the university against this agreement. Those years were not only years of drawing a balance sheet on the previous

115

period, of the causes for the defeat of João Goulart and our student leadership, but also years of organization and preparation to fight under new conditions against foreign domination.

In 1967 mass student mobilizations began and I got involved in them. I was elected to a position of leadership at the university. We called for the ending of the agreement with AID. That was when I was arrested for the first time. The military classified me as a student agitator, though all I had done was to discuss the absurdity of the agreement with some *compañeros* and propose that the students and professors should organize our own courses, our own political education in our university, according to the needs of our own country.

The struggles grew because at the same time a general discontent with the dictatorship was growing throughout Brazil, not only because of its surrender to U.S. interests, but also because of the frightful living conditions of the people and the ferocious repression that was unleashed against the students.

These important struggles culminated in 1968. During the previous three years the surrendering of the productive sectors of the economy controlled by national capital to imperialism had become so accentuated that these Brazilian-owned sectors of the economy were in a crisis. As a result, they even had to change the president, and Castelo Branco was replaced by Costa e Silva. Costa e Silva was supposed to be a humanist, a fellow who would understand the unrest, etc.

With the new government, our movement grew by leaps and bounds. The students flooded into the streets. There were intense mobilizations during 1968.

At the same time, the Brazilian middle class began to demonstrate. The union of bank workers was one of the most militant in this respect. Also some factories began to mobilize and there were even two strikes: the only strikes in Brazil since the 1964 coup. One was at Osasco in São Paulo, the other at Contagem in Minas Gerais.

At that time we elected a student delegation to address the most militant unions. And together with the workers we demonstrated. Our basic plank was to get the military out of the government, to get rid of imperialist penetration, and freedom for students to choose their administration and define their programs of study.

At that time — parallel to these direct actions in the streets, involving the unions along with the student sectors, bringing out the bank workers and other workers — a tremendous struggle began in Congress, which had just opened. The nationalist sectors threw themselves into a total and ferocious struggle against the military. With this situation, the government realized that however much the nationalist sectors had been damaged, it was impossible to grant them any type of concession. Or, to put it another way, if Costa e Silva had represented an attempt at negotiation with the nationalists, the military now realized that it could not engage in dialogue with them. It was at that time that the notorious Institutional Act No. 5 was published, which closed the recently opened Congress and deprived the federal court of its authority, transferring jurisdiction over all of society's decisions to the executive branch, i.e., to the military. At this point one of the cruelest repressive campaigns the world has ever seen was unleashed against the Brazilian people.

From then on I was quite seriously persecuted by the police. I had become an outlaw, that is to say, one of those being hunted down by the military.

In September 1968 the clandestine annual congress of the National Student Union (UNE) took place in Ibiúna, near São Paulo. Despite the fact that all the preparations were made with the utmost secrecy, the police discovered where we were and arrested eleven hundred students — the whole student vanguard that had arisen out of the struggles in Brazil. The eleven hundred students filled the jails of São Paulo. During the following weeks they were gradually released. Some, however, are still imprisoned. All told, twenty-three remained jailed. We who belonged to this twenty-three were destined to begin a long process of transfers from one prison to the next. I remember that we were in the Santo Amaro prison, then we went to the Tiradentes prison, then to Carandirú, until they took us to a military prison. Well, a quirk of fate occurred. Many Brazilian *compañeros* survived through such flukes. The police had separated us into groups of seven. I was transferred to a military prison near São Paulo and one of the *compañeros* with us was the son of the Minister of Tribunals. Two days before the military coup d'etat that overthrew Costa e Silva, the judge of a tribunal has issued a writ of habeus corpus for the twenty-three of us. But only the seven I was among succeeded in getting out. This minister, forseeing that there might be a coup, chartered a plane and went to the military prison where we were held and obtained our release twenty-five hours before the coup. Subsequently we were pursued on the road some 150 kilometers from São Paulo, since the military was put on total battle alert twenty-four hours before the coup began. We had been freed only an hour before the alert went into effect.

Well, it was with this coup on December 13, 1968, that the savage repression really began. Costa e Silva exits and the commanders-in-chief of the army, air force, and navy enter. They in turn later pass power on to Garrastazú Medici. The same night that the state of emergency was declared, University City was invaded. I had gone there, but I shouldn't have because after the news got out about the coup (this was in the morning), it was known that they would descend upon the university. However, I had problems during the day and had nowhere else to go when night fell. I had an intuition that they would invade University City that same night, and I was awakened at 3:00 a.m. by the sound of tanks. I was able to escape because it was raining heavily and there were ample thickets surrounding University City. I found a quagmire, a depression filled with water, and remained there covered with vegetation for four hours. Then I succeeded in reaching a friend's house. I had to go underground.

Starting with the beginning of 1969, the repression was extremely harsh. Many *compañeros* joined the armed struggle during that period. I didn't because I understood in those days that it was not the answer. Or, to put it more accurately, the military had succeeded in crushing the mass movement we had organized. Therefore from our place in the underground we needed to prepare another organizational phase. This meant linking our personal destinies, our political activity, to the mass movement and not setting ourselves up as small groups that would engage in armed struggle.

I was teaching under an assumed name in order to earn my daily bread. One day I looked through the window and saw I was surrounded by the police. There was no way to escape, and after my arrest I really went through a rough period. I was in prison a total of fifteen months. For seven of them I was kept incommunicado. I underwent various types of torture. I left prison with a foot fracture that still gives me trouble, but I succeeded in getting out, again through a freak occurrence. At that time I had three charges pending against me. So there was a quarrel over who would have jurisdiction between the civilian political police [the Department of Political and Social Order — DOPS] and the military, who were arrogant and showed no respect for civilian police seniority or hierarchical structures. In one of their frequent jurisdictional disputes over who would question me, the civilian police said, "No one is going to question him if I don't," and freed me on condition that I sign a document and show up every week to testify to the police. Of course I never returned.

I went then to stay in the home of some *compañeros*. Later I went to the north of the country where I lived on the ranch of some friends. At that time the Trotskyist party to which I belonged was practically crushed. Out of the six *compañeros* in the party leadership, two were imprisoned and subsequently died, two others were imprisoned but survived. Well, in this situation I had to keep myself isolated in order to struggle for survival because they had my name in all the police files and in the newspapers. I then moved further north under cover, and managed to get to the Bolivian border.

I entered Bolivia in October 1970, as it happened precisely at the time that Torres was assuming power. I got in touch with *compañeros* at the university there, and they welcomed me with open arms. There was an immense solidarity on the part of the students, who have an overall view and know all their country's problems. I was in Bolivia for a period of six months before going to Chile.

Bolivia is a country you really have to live in to get to know. One has to live alongside the people to know the contradictions of life there, to really know what poverty is — the subhuman conditions the people live in, the defensive way they act. The truth is there is such oppression by the authorities, and by Yankee imperialism, that people are held in a subhuman situation.

Bolivia was a great shock to me, a very important experience. I didn't spend my six months there as a tourist would. I stayed in Santa Cruz, in the east, for a short time, then in La Paz for a short while. But it was in the tin-mining center of Oruro that I had my most important experience.

Oruro had just lived through one of the most important struggles in Bolivia — the famous storming of the military bar-

racks there when Torres took over the reins of power. The
entire population had hurled itself against the barracks as
an act of repudiation of the military. Unarmed people—men,
women, children—threw themselves into the fray. About fifty
of them died. I participated in some of the meetings held by
the relatives of those who had been killed. I lived with these
people.

Earlier I mentioned that these people have a defensive life-
style. But that's only one side of the coin. When they reach
a certain point, they have a sense of self-sacrifice that is hardly
known in any other country. This is due to the very conditions
they live under. To put it simply, they have nothing to lose
because they don't even have a place to live. They live in the
town squares, in the streets. Those who, for example, eke out
a living selling their wares in the streets—maybe sweets, or
whatever they manage to produce—live in their curbside stalls
or under a tent on the sidewalks.

I worked for several months in the San José mine on the
outskirts of Oruro. But I could not continue because it seriously
undermined my health, which had already been damaged by
lack of medical care and eating a real meal only once every
three days in prison in Brazil.

After Allende took office I was able to enter Chile without
any documents and I applied for and received Chilean citizenship. I consciously went to Chile in order to get out of trouble
and to make my contribution to the Chilean people. But
basically, and paramount in my mind at that time if we're
going to be honest, I went to Chile looking for a little tran-
quility, a little repose which I had needed because of all the
tensions I had been living through. But I also wanted to inte-
grate myself with the Chilean people—to make my contribution.

I arrived in Chile in January 1971 and began working in
the area of civil engineering. The reception by the Chilean
people was incredible, the warmth and affection.

In this climate I began to advance professionally, and I
also got to know many *compañeros*. We began to discuss,
to exchange ideas on politics. These *compañeros* made it possible for me to again become politically involved, one of the
most important dynamic factors in my life. I got caught up
in the politics. I again became a part of the political life of my
comrades of the Fourth International and I engaged in com-
bining my professional activities (in order to earn my living)

with my political activities. And I remained involved in all of this until the day of the coup.

For months before the coup everyone in Chile knew a deci-,sive confrontation was coming, that a new coup would take place. But the Socialist and Communist parties had no orientation towards the danger, and many of the rank-and-file militants became very anxious, seeing that the government was doing nothing to strike at the right before it struck again. But they thought that on some level at least, the UP must be doing something to defend itself. In the first moments of the coup, even though I had been warning these militants that the line of the UP was impotent, I felt rather beaten down in the face of the verification of our prediction.

I lived very near the center of town. Everything was immediately surrounded by the army. There was a lot of shooting downtown and the planes began to arrive to bomb La Moneda. For me this was one of the saddest moments. I truly felt very saddened. A series of pictures passed through my memory — images of the massive demonstrations we had attended in these two and a half years, the militancy of the working class in these demonstrations. I recalled my work in the construction industry — I spent 80 percent of my time in direct contact with the workers — I remembered the meetings, the assemblies we had. I recalled the songs, like "We Shall Not Be Moved." All these scenes passed through my mind like a film. On the other hand, where were the revolutionary instructions the workers were desperately looking for? In the factories, in the streets, in the industrial *cordones*, in the unions, they were looking for this revolutionary orientation but did not get it.

Although I had witnessed three coups previously, during this one I was more politically conscious and I knew its implications. I grasped its full depth in those moments, witnessing the bombing of La Moneda, the traditional Moneda, so praised by the Socialists and Communists, by Allende, who never left the place when the masses called for his presence in the demonstrations they staged, in the struggles they engaged in, in the factories. He didn't leave La Moneda. Well, at least he was consistent, because he died there. At that moment, however much I had opposed the leaderships of these parties, however much I knew their responsibility for the defeat, at that moment felt in common cause with them. I also felt sad to see how these leaders were being beaten — how they were chasing these leaders as if they were rats. Although I didn't agree with any of them in their political line, in those moments I felt in solidarity with them.

I tried to get past the downtown sections but didn't succeed. I had to cross through the center of town to get to a friend's house in order to be more protected, because I knew my house was going to be raided by the police as I was pretty well known.

I tried to get across the center of town and failed because there was heavy crossfire. At one point I was forced to seek safety under a car. I returned home and was unable to do a thing because no one could leave. The curfew was extended through Tuesday and Wednesday afternoon. I was at the home of some neighbors. We were playing ping-pong when the police burst in. They put me against the wall and began kicking me. They demanded my papers and, what is interesting, they asked, "Where are the two Brazilians?" I replied, "No, there is only one Brazilian and that's me." Well, they smashed up the contents of the entire house, but they didn't break the tape recorder, camera, or typewriter, and the official kept the house keys so he could come back and take everything. And sure enough, these things were later taken. However, he broke the refrigerator — the only thing of any value which remained — broke the windows. I had little money but of course it was taken from me. They even took the tooth paste and also a necktie the official liked. Well, they took me to the interrogation room of the *carabineros*, inflicting beatings on me. Of course I was sure I wouldn't escape alive. I was in the interrogation chamber facing twenty cops. They put me face down on the floor — I was the mat. They trampeled me, hit me with the butts of their carbines and machine guns. Well, when I went downstairs in front of the police station, they made me run. They told me they were going to kill me, told me to run fifty meters. I, as if punch drunk, began walking. I was walking, nothing more. They told me to stop and enter the police station. There I was lucky. Why? Because I had Chilean citizenship. I was Chilean, although obviously a Brazilian. Because I had my papers in order. I had recently been released from a long stay in the hospital, and the commander of the police station wasn't an aggressive type. He even asked me a series of things in a friendly manner. I spoke of my illness and everything. However, when the commander left, two officials showed up and gave me a complete working over. They beat me in an incredible manner that I could not understand. Well, I can understand it, but one of the things that leaves me psychologically depressed is the capacity that these people have to administer beatings. I remained motionless and was beaten as if I were a rock or something.

Well, I was there a while (an hour and a half, more or less). I'm going to describe a very important scene. When I got to the police station, there were ten *compañeros* seated, their heads dripping with blood. They were all bloodied up. They were totally unrecognizable — even if one of them were one's best friend. And the following dialogue took place between a captain and the lieutenant: "Well, what are we going to do with these elements? Why don't we kill them?" "Let's not kill them because they were unarmed." "Well, killing them is better than leaving them in this state. We can't take them to headquarters in this state. What are we going to do with them?" The lieutenant remained silent and his superior said, "Well, leave them to me." After the lapse of half an hour, he departed with these ten "elements"; surely they were executed. These ten were arrested on the San Cristóbal hill, which is located in the center of the city and where a large arms cache was discovered.

After an hour and a half of being constantly clubbed, they took me to a cell even though all my papers were in order. On the following day, after twelve hours in the police station, I was released. I couldn't believe it, but I was free. I believe it was basically due to this commander. I was released, but during the curfew. And I didn't give any type of reaction (this is very important). Any reaction on my part would have meant my death. Because these people were not interested in prisoners at this time; they were only interested in death. Well, they had beat me, made me strip off all my cloths, even gave me asthma attacks (I'm asthmatic) but of what concern was this to them — finally, every imaginable type of provocation. Had I reacted, it would have meant my death. I didn't speak, it was not my first experience in this. I simply remained quiet, accepting every outrage. Well, I was then released during the curfew. During the curfew anyone who is found is killed. I even thought that they were going to shoot me down there, because of the curfew. At all the police stations there is a guard — they are cordoned off, and I thought he would shoot me when I got to the street. When I reached the corner I saw a lady looking out the window; she evidently saw that I had the look of someone who was terrified and had spent the whole night without sleep. She glimpsed my scared face and immediately realized I was coming from the police station. I turned to her, begging asylum in her home, telling her that I had just left police headquarters and that I couldn't be wandering around the streets, asking her to let me stay there until I could return home. She agreed and we talked until the curfew was over (approximately ten hours).

I went home and immediately phoned a friend. I returned home only to collect my other identification papers, which could protect me. I then got in contact with some friends. We discussed what was to be done and decided to contact some *compañeros* from our little group and to meet somewhere to apply the course of action we had agreed upon: to get into an embassy or, failing this, to cross the border somewhere in the south. We worked on this for a week. We were shut up in the house with three other *compañeros*. One of the *compañeras* could leave, and she was the one who made all the contacts. The two of us who were foreigners could not go out into the streets because we would immediately be discovered. You see I'm a typical Brazilian type and am spotted as Brazilian anywhere. And the other *compañero* couldn't open his mouth because of his strong Argentine accent.

One morning plans were completed and a friend came in a car to take us to an embassy.